EXPLORING

Solent **Blue Line**

COUNTRY

· A PAST and PRESENT COMPANION ·

50	SOUTHAMPTON—LOWER UPHAM—BISHOP'S WALTHAM—PETERSFIELD.	50
'8.5.53	(For additional journeys between Southampton and Bishop's Waltham see Services 51 and 51A.) Light figures denote a.m. times. Dark figures denote p.m. times.	

		NSu	NSu									Su								
Southampton (Bus Station)	dep	6 0	8 0	10 0	12 0	12 0	2 0	4 0	6 0	7 0	8 0		9 45	...	...	...	...	...	...	...
Bitterne (Red Lion)	,,	6 12	8 12	10 12	12 12	12 12	2 12	4 12	6 12	7 12	8 12		9 57	...	...	...	...	...	...	...
Moorgreen Hospital	,,	6 24	8 24	10 24	12 24	12 24	2 24	4 24	6 24	7 24	8 24		10 9	...	...	...	...	...	...	...
Moorgreen (Soton Arms)	,,	6 26	8 26	10 26	12 26	12 26	2 26	4 26	6 26	7 26	8 26		10 11	...	...	...	...	...	...	...
Horton Hth. (Denhams Cnr.)	,,	6 30	8 30	10 30	12 30	12 30	2 30	4 30	6 30	7 30	8 30		10 15	...	...	...	...	...	...	...
Drayton	,,	D 8 35	10 35	12 35	12 35	2 35	4 35	6 35	7 35	8 35		10 20	...	...	...	...	...	...	...	...
Fair Oak (Square)	,,	...	8 42	10 42	12 42	12 42	2 42	4 42	6 42	7 42	8 42		10 27	...	...	...	...	...	...	...
Lower Upham (Alma Inn)	,,	6 44	8 50	10 50	12 50	12 50	2 50	4 50	6 50	7 50	8 50		10 35	...	...	...	...	...	...	...
Bishop's Waltham	,,	6 33	8 38	10 38	12 38	12 38	2 38	4 58	6 58	7 58	8 58		...	...	...	...	...	...	...	...
Swanmore (Church)	,,	7 0	9 5	11 5	1 5	1 5	3 5	5 5	5 7	5 8	5 9	5	...	...	...	...	...	...	...	...
Droxford (Fire Station)	,,	7 7	9 12	11 12	1 12	1 23	3 12	5 12	5 17	12 8	12 9	12	...	...	...	...	...	...	...	...
Corhampton (Post Office)	,,	7 15	9 20	11 20	1 20	3 20	5 20	7 20	7 26	8 26	9 20	...	...	...	...	...	...	...	...	...
Warnford (George Inn)	,,	7 25	9 25	11 25	1 25	3 25	5 25	7 25	8 25	9 25	25·	...	...	...	...	...	...	...	...	...
West Meon (Thomas Lord)	,,	7 31	9 31	11 31	1 31	3 31	5 31	7 31	8 31	31	...	9 31	...	...	...	...	...	...	...	...
Drayton	,,	7 35	9 35	11 35	1 35	3 35	5 35	7 35	8 35	...	9 35	...	...	...	...	...	...	...	...	...
East Meon	,,	7 43	9 43	11 43	1 43	3 43	5 43	7 43	8 43	...	9 43	...	...	...	...	...	...	...	...	...
Langrish (Post Office)	,,	7 47	9 47	11 47	1 47	5 47	7 47	7 47	8 47	...	9 47	...	...	...	...	...	...	...	...	...
Stroud (Post Office)	,,	7 55	9 55	11 55	1 55	3 55	5 55	7 55	8 55	...	9 55	...	...	...	...	...	...	...	...	...
Petersfield (Square)	arr																			

		NSu	NSu									Su								
Petersfield (Square)	dep	6 50	8 0	10 0	12 0	12 0	2 0	4 0	0 6	0 8	0 9	0·	...	...	...					
Stroud (Post Office)	,,	6 58	8 8	10 8	12 8	2 8	8 4	8 6	8 8	8 9	8	...	...	...						
Langrish (Post Office)	,,	7 2	8 12	10 12	12 12	2 12	2 12	4 12	12 6	12 8	12 9	12	...	...	...					
East Meon	,,	7 10	8 20	10 20	12 20	2 20	4 20	6 20	8 20	9 20	...	...	...							
Drayton	,,	7 14	8 24	10 24	12 24	12 24	2 24	4 24	6 24	8 24	9 24	...	...	...		Su—Sunday only.					
West Meon (Thomas Lord)	,,	7 20	8 30	10 30	12 30	2 30	4 30	6 30	8 30	9 30	9 30	...	...	NSu—Not Sunday.							
Warnford (George Inn)	,,	7 25	8 35	10 35	12 35	2 35	4 35	6 35	8 35	...	9 35	...	...	D—Via Durley.							
Corhampton (Post Office)	,,	7 33	8 43	10 43	12 43	2 43	4 43	6 43	8 43	...	9 43	...	...								
Droxford (Fire Station)	,,	7 40	8 50	10 50	12 50	2 50	4 50	6 50	8 50	...	9 50	...	...	E—Via Eastleigh, North							
Swanmore (Church)	,,	6 27	7 47	8 57	10 57	12 57	2 57	4 57	6 57	8 57	...	9 57	...	Stoneham and Bassett.							
Bishop's Waltham	,,	6 35	7 55	9 5	11 5	1 5	5 3	5 5	5 7	5 9	5	...	10 5	...	†—To Southampton Docks.						
Lower Upham (Alma Inn)	,,	...	9 13	11 13	1 13	3 13	5 13	7 13	9 13	13	...	10 13	...	...							
Fair Oak (Square)	,,	D D 9 20	11 20	1 20	3 20	5 20	7 20	9 20	20	...	10 20	...	...								
Horton Hth. (Denhams Cr.)	,,	6 49	8 9 9 25	11 25	1 25	3 25	5 25	7 25	9 25	25	...	10 25	...	...							
Moorgreen (Soton Arms)	,,	6 53	E 9 29	11 29	1 29	3 29	5 29	7 29	9 29	29	...	10 29	...	...							
Moorgreen Hospital	,,	6 55	...	9 31	11 31	1 31	3 31	5 31	7 31	9 31	...	10 31	...	...							
Bitterne (Red Lion)	,,	7 7	...	9 43	11 43	1 43	3 43	5 43	7 43	9 43	...	10 43	...	...							
Southampton (Bus Station)	arr	7 17	19 9	0 9	9 55	11 55	1 55	3 55	5 55	7 55	9 55	...	10 55	...							

1953

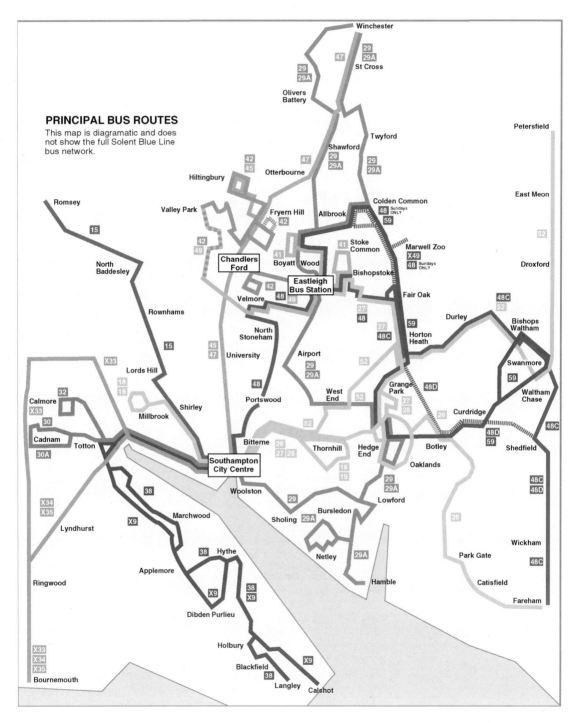

PRINCIPAL BUS ROUTES

This map is diagramatic and does not show the full Solent Blue Line bus network.

2001

EXPLORING

Solent
Blue Line
COUNTRY

·A PAST and PRESENT COMPANION·

Chris Harris

·TOWN AND COUNTRY HERITAGE·
from
The NOSTALGIA Collection

First published in 2002

British Library Cataloguing in Publication Data

A catalogue record for this book is available from the British Library.

ISBN 1 85895 185 2

Past & Present Publishing Ltd
The Trundle
Ringstead Road
Great Addington
Kettering
Northants NN14 4BW

Tel/Fax: 01536 330588
email: sales@nostalgiacollection.com
Website: www.nostalgiacollection.com

Printed and bound in Great Britain

┌─────────────┐
│ **Past** and │
│ **Present** │
└─────────────┘

A Past & Present book
from
The **NOSTALGIA** *Collection*

Acknowledgements

T his book has only been made possible by the help that has been generously and cheerfully given by a number of people.

I thank Solent Blue Line's Commercial Manager, Philip Curtis, for his agreement that the book could be produced using that Company's corporate identity, and for the photograph of Solent Blue Line's latest type of double-deck bus on display at the 2001 Coach and Bus Show.

Dave and Betty Underwood of Classic Pictures in Christchurch have again very kindly allowed me to reproduce photographs from their stock, and this has provided an interesting nucleus of general views.

Transport historian (and former busman) Brian Jackson from Weymouth has kindly supplied many photographs from his collection covering all forms of transport, and has provided valuable information for captions, while another former busman, Peter Trevaskis from Normandy, Guildford, has allowed me to use a number of photographs from his Aldershot & District Bus Interest Group collection.

Once again Wilts & Dorset's collection of old photographs dating back to the Hants & Dorset days has been raided, and I am grateful to Operations Director Andrew Bryce for permission to use these and for his encouragement and help with this project.

Thanks also to Lloyd Lay of White Horse Ferries for permission to use the view of Hythe Pier; to Nigel Wood of the Lingwood Netley Hospital Archive for the photographs of the old Royal Victoria Hospital; to David Harvey from Dudley for the photograph of Southampton tram No 39; and to Peter Drew of Hants & Dorset Trim for the interior view of SRU 981. Tim Foster again showed interest in the project and took the 2001 photograph of Southampton Town Quay on page 15. Vin Almond of Pindar, Preston, kindly agreed to supply the map.

Many other people have supplied helpful information, including Philip Davies from Ferndown, Peter Allen from Poole, Nancy Knight, formerly of Poole Hospital, and Sue Tapliss of Eastleigh Museum. To these and to others who have supplied useful snippets of knowledge, my very grateful thanks.

Contents

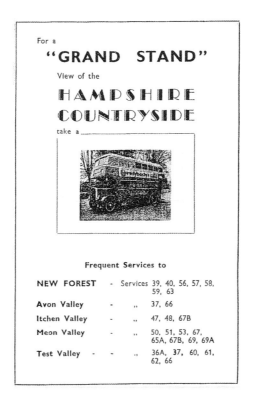

For a

"GRAND STAND"

View of the

HAMPSHIRE COUNTRYSIDE

take a _____

Frequent Services to

NEW FOREST	- Services	39, 40, 56, 57, 58, 59, 63
Avon Valley	- ,,	37, 66
Itchen Valley	- ,,	47, 48, 67B
Meon Valley	- ,,	50, 51, 53, 67, 65A, 67B, 69, 69A
Test Valley	- - ,,	36A, 37, 60, 61, 62, 66

1948

These two very pleasant views epitomise Southampton in the 1960s. In the first Hants & Dorset Bristol LD6B fleet number 1416 (XEL 550) is seen arriving at Southampton Bus Station with a Service 47 journey from Winchester on 21 July 1966. This vehicle entered service in June 1959 and was withdrawn in October 1975. The Bus Station building was designed to complement the Civic Centre opposite, and lasted from 1933 until 1987 – see also page 9.

The Civic Centre is illustrated in the lower photograph, which was taken around 1960, and shows a lowbridge-bodied Bristol KSW6B on a mid-afternoon eastbound journey. The Civic Centre building, opened by the Duke of York in 1932, has changed very little in appearance over the years; apart from the vehicles and the fashions the view from this point is very similar more than 40 years later. Note the schoolboy in uniform blazer carrying his satchel of homework! *Aldershot & District Bus Interest Group/Wilts & Dorset collection*

Introduction

In 1999 I had the great pleasure of *Exploring Wilts & Dorset Country*, compiling a collection of photographs taken from the 1900s to the 1960s and matching them with modern photographs of the same locations.

During 2001 I travelled further east and undertook the same exercise, with similar enjoyment, in the area served by Solent Blue Line buses. In this book photographs taken between 1900 and 1982 are paired with photographs taken of the same locations in 2001, and once again the final chapter illustrates some milestones in the development of all forms of transport in the area. Whether you have nostalgic memories of the area as it was in days gone by, or if you wonder what various places looked like years ago, this book should be of interest.

Solent Blue Line commenced operations in Southampton on 25 May 1987, with three crew-operated cross-city routes. Considerable expansion came in October 1987 when the Stagecoach Hampshire Bus operations, based in Southampton and Eastleigh, were sold to Solent Blue Line, and the Company also acquired the Hants & Sussex operation from Basil Williams.

The area covered by this book is therefore centred on Southampton and Eastleigh, together with the Waterside area, and routes to Winchester, Romsey, Netley, Hamble, Petersfield and Fareham. All of the locations included are served by Solent Blue Line buses, but it is fair to say that in some instances (for example Romsey, Winchester and Fareham) they are also served by other operators. Nonetheless they are important destinations on the Solent Blue Line network, and the general geography of the area is such that it would be wrong not to include them here.

Although the company name Solent Blue Line is of comparatively recent origin, its 'family connections' via the October 1987 acquisition of part of Hampshire Bus go back much further. A number of the routes operated can be traced back to the days of Hants & Dorset Motor Services, which ran buses in the area from 1920 until 1983 and with whom I began my career in the bus industry at Poole Depot almost 30 years ago. Subsequently, during the late 1970s and early 1980s, I worked in what was then Hants & Dorset's Eastern Area, both on the Market Analysis Project and with the Company's mobile publicity unit – illustrated on page 26. Linking this with my extensive travels in the area as a teenager during the 1960s, I have been privileged to have seen for myself some of the changes illustrated in this book.

As well as the historic link to Hants & Dorset, Solent Blue Line has from the beginning been a wholly owned subsidiary of Southern Vectis, which operates the bus services on the Isle of Wight. Southern Vectis has, of course, a distinguished history stretching back to the 1920s, and I hope to feature that company's area in another in this series of Past and Present explorations.

Compiling *Exploring Solent Blue Line Country* has been most enjoyable; I hope you will gain similar enjoyment from reading the book.

Chris Harris
Poole, Dorset

Before we start exploring Solent Blue Line Country past and present, let us compare the vehicles we could use for our travels. Representing the 'past' era we have Hants & Dorset fleet number 949 (LJ 5019), at Eastleigh station on 12 August 1953. This 1932 Leyland TD2 had been rebodied by Beadle and fitted with a Gardner 5LW diesel engine in February 1944. The opening vents in the top-deck front windows and the three-aperture destination display seen here were put in during April 1950. LJ 5019 was withdrawn in October 1954 and passed to a showman, with whom it was observed still in use in Sunderland ten years later.

In contrast we see one of Solent Blue Line's latest double deck-buses at the time of writing. One of an order for eight Volvo B7TL buses with East Lancs low-floor Myllennium Vyking bodywork, it is pictured on display at the Coach and Bus Show held at the National Exhibition Centre, Birmingham, in October 2001. *Brian Jackson collection/Solent Blue Line*

Southampton

SOUTHAMPTON BUS STATION at West Marlands was officially opened on Monday 23 January 1933 by the Chairman of the Traffic Commissioners, Southern Area, Sir Reginald Ford. The building was designed in a classical style to be in keeping with the contemporary Civic Centre opposite (see also page 6). The 'past' photograph was taken on 14 December 1953 and illustrates this handsome bus station in its halcyon days. On the left of the photograph can be seen the Grand Theatre, built in 1898. Sadly this closed on 31 October 1959 and was demolished in March 1960. Shops and an office block in a very 1960s style were built there shortly afterwards; this building can be glimpsed on the left of the 'present' photograph, taken on Saturday 24 March 2001.

Southampton Bus Station was demolished in 1987 and the Marlands Shopping Centre was built on the site; buses now terminate at a number of roadside stands around the City Centre. Unfortunately the rose garden has been removed from the middle of Civic Centre Road, and with the amount of traffic using the road in 2001 guard rails and a pelican crossing are necessary. *Wilts & Dorset collection/CH*

GROSVENOR SQUARE: With the purchase of Tourist Motor Coaches of Southampton in May 1935, Hants & Dorset acquired a large site in Grosvenor Square that extended through to Bedford Place. On the Bedford Place side of the site the Company built a coach station (illustrated on page 90 of *Exploring Wilts & Dorset Country*) and a tours booking office, with offices above, which later became Hants & Dorset's Eastern Area Schedules Office. The majority of the ground was used to build a large bus garage fronting onto Grosvenor Square in what was then a very modern design. The building was completed in 1938, and is seen in the 'past' photograph in 1946 – only eight years old but showing signs of damage from bomb blast during the Second World War. Someone with a tidy mind must have lined up the buses – in the first doorway is a quartet of Leyland TD3s delivered between March and August 1935, while in the second we see four Bristol K5Gs, which entered service between June 1938 and April 1940.

After the break-up of Hants & Dorset in 1983 the premises at Grosvenor Square were subsequently sold for development, and a casual visitor today would have no clue that a large bus depot once stood where this office block now stands, as seen on Saturday 24 March 2001. *S. A. Chandler & Co (Wilts & Dorset collection)/CH*

SOUTHAMPTON CENTRAL STATION: When the line from Southampton to Dorchester was opened in 1847, a small station was provided a little way to the east of the present Southampton Central station. Initially known as Blechynden, and renamed Southampton West in 1858, this small station was soon found to be inadequate for the traffic being handled, and a much larger replacement station was opened on the present site in November 1895. In 1935 this was further enlarged on the 'down' side with buildings to the Southern Railway's latest design in concrete, although the 1895 buildings on the 'up' side remained unchanged. A new footbridge was provided and the station was renamed Southampton Central. Sadly Southampton Central station was badly damaged by air raids during the Second World War, and in particular a section of the 1935 building on the 'down' platform was blown to pieces when two parachute land-mines fell on the station on 22 July 1941. The 'past' photograph dates from September 1953 and nicely illustrates the 1895 buildings on the 'up' side complete with their distinctive

clock tower, together with the 1935 concrete footbridge. The shortened canopy on the island platform is a still-visible scar from the 1941 air raid. Note the water columns for steam locomotives at the head of the two 'up' platforms, with the rather attractive heater to prevent the column on the island platform from freezing during frosty weather.

The 1895 buildings on the 'up' side were demolished in 1966 and replaced by the office block seen in the 'present' view, taken on Saturday 1 September 2001. The line was electrified in 1967 and all of the platform lines can now be worked in either direction, resulting in the signal gantry right across the foreground. *Brian Jackson collection/CH*

PROSPECT PLACE: These photographs show the junction of Above Bar Street and Commercial Road, Southampton, in 1908 and 2001. In the right foreground of the 1908 photograph a number of people can be seen outside Plummer Roddis Ltd, no doubt looking for bargains in the well-advertised sale! This drapery business was founded in Eastbourne in 1873 by William Plummer and, as confirmed by the sign on the wall of the shop, soon expanded with branches in a number of towns; the Southampton shop opened in 1896. Badly damaged by bombing in 1940, the premises were rebuilt in 1958. Now occupied by the Southampton Institute, the building was renamed Sir James Matthews House in 1994 in recognition of a local benefactor.

The attractive clock tower in the centre background of the 'past' view was built in 1889. Designed by S. K. Pope, it was provided from a bequest of £1,000 from a Mrs Henrietta Bellenden Sayers. In 1934 it was dismantled and moved to Bitterne Park Triangle to allow road improvements to take place in Above Bar Street. Traffic was so light in 1908 that passengers for the tram to Bitterne Park could safely wait in the middle of the road.

On the left of the photographs the handsome buildings of Prospect Place, already used commercially in 1908, had long gone by 2001. The present building was erected in 1957 for Tyrrell & Green, whose original department store had been destroyed during the Second World War. This outlet now trades as John Lewis in Southampton's West Quay shopping centre, and when photographed the 1957 premises were disused. Closer to the camera, the Old Fat Cat public house was built in the early 1960s as offices and showrooms for the Southern Gas Board; the building was converted to its present use in 1996. *Classic Pictures/CH*

ABOVE BAR STREET: Here we compare the scene looking northwards along Above Bar Street in the late 1950s and on Saturday 24 March 2001. The Tyrrell & Green department store building can be seen in the centre of the photographs and fixes the location in relation to the views shown opposite. It will be noticed in the 'past' view that the Gas Board premises (now the Old Fat Cat) had not yet been built – at that time a wool shop occupied the site. There is still a building society on the corner of New Road, but the premises have been completely rebuilt. Changes to the buildings on the left will also be noted.

The attractive shelter on the right has been replaced by a more functional but nonetheless stylish modern design, while a shelter has been provided for the bus stop in the left foreground. It is pleasing to see a number of intending passengers waiting for buses here in both views. The group of K6 telephone kiosks, just visible behind the tree in the 'past' photograph, has been replaced by a group of kiosks sited closer to the roadside; these are of the modern KX100 type, a design first introduced in 1985 and now more common than the traditional type. The

traffic lights at the crossroads will be noted; at the time of the 'past' photograph this was the intersection of two main routes, the A33 and the A3024, and the standard trunk-road-style direction signs of the era can be seen. Also of interest is the additional sign showing the way to London (77 miles); signs of this type were found at various locations on the way to London until around 1970. Traffic schemes in Southampton have resulted in this crossroads now being used mainly by vehicles making local journeys, both the A33 and A3024 having been re-routed away from this bustling city centre location.
Wilts & Dorset collection/CH

SOUTHAMPTON HIGH STREET: The south side of Southampton's famous Bargate can be seen in the background of both of these photographs of the High Street, taken looking north from a point near the junction with Bernard Street. Dating from the 12th century and the principal entrance to the medieval walled settlement, all traffic still had to pass through the Bargate at the time of the 'past' photograph, taken around 1910. However, even in the early years of the 20th century this constriction of the traffic flow was causing congestion, and (amazingly) there were even suggestions that the Bargate should be demolished! Happily this did not happen, but some adjoining properties and parts of the old walls were taken down to enable a roadway to be provided on the east side of the Bargate in 1932 and on the west side in 1938. The Bargate can be seen thus isolated from the surrounding buildings in the 'present' photograph, taken on Saturday 24 March 2001.

Electric trams operated in Southampton from 1900 until 1949; an early tramcar with back-to-back 'knifeboard' seating on the open upper deck is seen on its way to Southampton Common (see also page 94). Beyond it the west side of Southampton High Street was to suffer severely in the Second World War, and the rather plain and austere replacement structures can be contrasted with the former elegant buildings, most of which were lost during the air raids. Fortunately more of the buildings on the eastern side of the road have survived. Of particular note is

the Dolphin Hotel, whose origins go back to the 15th century and whose distinctive frontage with its large bay windows dates from around 1760. The church spire behind it in the 'past' view belonged to St Lawrence's Church. This was demolished in 1925, having been declared redundant owing to changing population patterns. *Classic Pictures/CH*

14

TOWN QUAY: It is the corner of the former Harbour Board building, dating from 1925 and seen on the left of both views, that confirms that these two photographs were taken from the same point. When the 'past' photograph was taken in September 1953 considerable coastal freight traffic was handled at Southampton's Town Quay, which was then served by a railway line as part of a well-used network in the Docks area. Locomotive No 30588, seen shunting trucks, was originally built as a 2-2-0 locomotive by the London & South Western Railway in 1906, and was one of a batch of small locomotives intended for lightweight local trains. Initially used on services between Southampton and Winchester, during 1915 it was hauling workmen's trains between Bournemouth West and the Royal Naval Cordite Factory under construction at Holton Heath, then in 1917 it was employed on shunting in Portsmouth Dockyard.

Far from suitable for this work, the locomotive was rebuilt as a 0-4-0 tank engine in 1922, and in this form it was mainly employed at Southampton Town Quay until withdrawal in December 1957. Railway freight working at the Town Quay ended in May 1970.

This part of Southampton has been redeveloped, with a marina (seen in the background of the 'present' photograph, taken on Saturday 9 June 2001), offices and restaurants – the atmosphere of the area has completely changed. *Brian Jackson collection/Tim Foster*

SIX DIALS was the name given to the meeting point of New Road, St Andrew's Road, St Mary's Road, St Mark's Road, Northam Road and St Mary Street in the Kingsland area of Southampton. These photographs capture the view looking west along Northam Road in 1913 and on Saturday 9 June 2001. Only one building remains standing today – the Bridge Tavern on the corner of St Mary Street on the left. In 1913 this was owned by Forder's Brewery, but became a Brickwood's house in 1925 and subsequently passed to Whitbread in 1971. It closed as a public house in 1982 and became the Bridge Gallery, but in the early 1990s this moved to premises in Bedford Place, and the former Bridge Tavern is now used for residential purposes.

Northam Road was part of the main A3024 road into Southampton, and as traffic built up after the Second World War Six Dials became a point of serious congestion. For a number of years a one-way system was in operation, with only westbound traffic entering Southampton along Northam Road at this point, while eastbound traffic left the city via Brintons Road. By the 1980s this gyratory system was itself something of a bottleneck, and the A3024 was subsequently realigned as a dual carriageway, just out of sight behind the bushes on the right of the 2001 photograph. This part of Northam Road is now used by two-way local traffic. The tower crane in the centre background heralds the construction of another new building, emphasising Southampton's constantly changing cityscape. *Classic Pictures/CH*

FOUNDRY LANE takes its name from a foundry established here in the early 19th century by Charles and Henry Tickell. Taken over by Alexander Fletcher and John Young in 1824, it was then bought by Ogle & Summers, who moved from Whitechapel, East London, in 1831. By the late 1830s the foundry's activities had turned increasingly towards shipbuilding, although its location was less than ideal for this, and accordingly the company developed a new site on the River Itchen at Northam, the premises in Foundry Lane closing in 1854. Large-scale house-building in this area commenced in 1853 and continued for the rest of the 19th century, the buildings seen in these photographs being constructed during this period. The views are separated by a period of around 95 years, but the location is instantly recognisable; very few changes have been made to the houses.

Two boys in the left foreground of the 'past' photograph display 1906 fashions for lads; 12-year-old Tim Foster demonstrates modern designer wear for young gentlemen on Saturday 9 June 2001. The big difference between the two pictures is, of course, the parked cars; when these houses were designed and built nobody could have foreseen the high level of car ownership that would prevail more than 100 years later. *Classic Pictures/CH*

SWAYTHLING STATION was opened on 15 October 1883, 44 years after the line on which it is located. Constructed by a local building firm, the main buildings are on the 'down' side. The station was designed so that the line could easily be upgraded to quadruple track, the buildings being situated some way back from the platform and linked to it by a covered walkway; if four tracks had been installed it would have been a simple matter to move the platform back without the need for modifications to the main buildings. The 'past' photograph, dating from around 1920, clearly shows this unusual layout. A bomb penetrated the Booking Office in January 1941, and made such a mess that it was thought to have exploded and, in keeping with the spirit of the time, business continued as usual. Fortunately the landlord of a nearby public house intervened, saying that he was sure the bomb had *not* exploded – the station was then evacuated and a disposal team searched for and removed the unexploded bomb!

The line was electrified in 1967, but in many ways the view in 2001 is very similar to that of around 80 years earlier. The main buildings and platform shelters survive, although the shed, converted from an old van body, has gone. Modern lighting and colour light signalling have been installed, but a traveller from years ago would still easily recognise the place. *Classic Pictures/CH*

Eastleigh

EASTLEIGH BUS STATION: Although a depot had existed in Blenheim Road for a number of years previously, services did not start using Eastleigh Bus Station until 1959. Prior to that time the focal point for Hants & Dorset buses in Eastleigh had been the railway station, as illustrated on page 20. The bus station consisted of this row of departure stands between Southampton Road and Market Street, parallel with the south side of Blenheim Road. The 'past' view shows the premises when newly opened in 1959, and is taken from Southampton Road looking towards Market Street. Waiting to depart from Stand F is fleet number 1249 (JEL 267), a Bristol K5G with Eastern Coach Works lowbridge bodywork new in March 1950. Other lowbridge Bristol Ks can be seen parked on the right.

Eastleigh Bus Station was only at this location for 17 years; in July 1976 it was moved to Upper Market Street (with Portakabin offices for the first few years). The operational depot remained at Blenheim Road for a little longer before being moved to Barton Park (see pages 24-27). The 'present' photograph was taken from the same location on Saturday 28 April 2001. A house has been built where the entrance to the bus station used to be, and a visitor to the area would find little to indicate the site's former use. However, in this instance the change has been an improvement for bus passengers in that the new location in Upper Market Street is closer to the Town Centre and the railway station. *Wilts & Dorset collection/CH*

EASTLEIGH STATION was opened on this site in 1841, two years after the opening of the railway between Winchester and Southampton. The station was known as Bishopstoke until 1899, when it became Eastleigh & Bishopstoke, finally becoming just Eastleigh in 1923. The 'past' photograph was taken on 8 January 1954 and shows the station entrance building constructed in 1875; to reach the trains it was necessary to cross the footbridge to the two island platforms. Outside the station entrance Hants & Dorset fleet number 1255 (JEL 274), a Bristol K5G with 55-seat Eastern Coach Works lowbridge bodywork and new in April 1950, is ready for the next departure to Woolston on Service 49. A queue of passengers wearing winter overcoats can be seen in front of the delightful ornate wooden bus waiting room, built by Twinn Brothers of Pokesdown in the 1930s. Traffic was light enough in January 1954 for a motor car to be parked against the traffic flow on Southampton Road; note the very basic windscreen heater and the way the radiator is protected against the cold. Ind Coope's beers were available at the Junction Hotel seen in the background.

The abolition of the up loop line made it possible to remodel Eastleigh station with a level entrance to the remaining up platform in 1990. The unusual chimney stack on the station roof proves that both photographs were taken from the same location, and it can be seen how part of the footbridge has been removed and the station entrance moved back from the road to create a car parking area. The increase in road traffic is very apparent in the 2001 photograph; yellow lines now prohibit roadside parking on Southampton Road, while in the background the Junction Hotel has long been demolished. *Wilts & Dorset collection/CH*

SOUTHAMPTON ROAD, EASTLEIGH: These photographs are taken from a point a little to the north of those opposite, and are looking in the other direction; the Junction Hotel in the left foreground of the 'past' view fixes the location. The 'past' photograph dates from the late 1920s; notice the prominent signage on the station canopy, a product of the publicity department of the Southern Railway that was formed in 1923. Beyond the station entrance can be seen 'The Elms' which dated from 1841 and was the first house (of many) to be built for the London & South Western Railway in Eastleigh. Sadly it is now demolished.

The appearance of the Home Tavern in the right foreground of both photographs has changed little. This building dates from 1887 and replaces an earlier thatched inn, also called the Home Tavern, on the same spot. What was the National Provincial Bank on the opposite corner of Leigh Road has now become the NatWest, as it is known today, but the exterior of the building is virtually unchanged. Beyond the bank in the 'past' photograph are some small shops, then 'Tate's Terrace', a row of houses built for railway workers by a Fareham builder called Tate. Both the shops and the terrace have been demolished and replaced by blocks of offices, as can be seen in the present photograph, taken on Saturday 28 April 2001. *Classic Pictures/CH*

LEIGH ROAD, EASTLEIGH: The section of Leigh Road between the High Street and Market Street is an important part of Eastleigh's town centre shopping area. The 'past' photograph was taken around 1930 and shows this pleasant street with buildings dating mainly from the late Victorian period. Part of the distinctive Eagle Building can be seen in the right foreground; Woolworth's still occupy the centre section in 2001, although this part of the original building was demolished and replaced by a modern structure during the early 1960s. Further along, what was Baker's outfitters on the corner of Market Street is now a chemist's shop; much of the upper part of the building remains, but the delightful tower has been lost.

This section of the street has now been pedestrianised, with attractive paving and a stylish canopy in front of the shops, complete with flower baskets. As can be seen in the photograph taken on Monday 20 August 2001 it is a popular place to shop; on Thursdays and Saturdays a lively market is held here with bustling stalls in the space formerly occupied by the roadway. Notice the ornate clock by the junction with Market Street, to the left of which is a Solent Blue Line bus turning into Upper Market where the present Eastleigh Bus Station is located, replacing former premises near Blenheim Road (see also page 19). *Classic Pictures/CH*

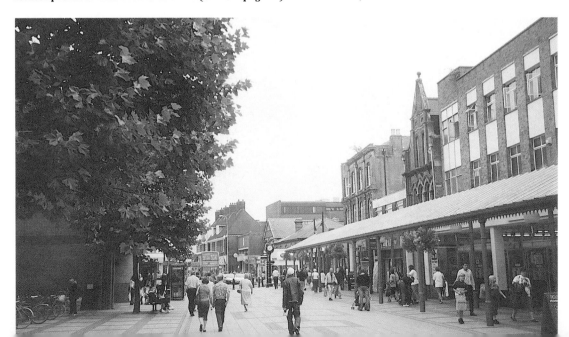

EASTLEIGH RECREATION GROUND was acquired by the Local Authority in 1896 and laid out as grassland with paths, trees and shrubs to provide an area of open space for the residents of what was by then a fast-growing town. In the 'past' photograph we see people enjoying this amenity, probably around 1910. During the First World War huts were erected on the Recreation Ground and used as a military hospital for casualties returning from the war in France. In the Second World War sub-surface air-raid shelters were created there by excavating the grass areas.

The modern photograph, taken during the afternoon of Saturday 28 April 2001, shows that the Recreation Ground is still appreciated by Eastleigh's townsfolk. An excellent children's playground has been created in recent years; some of the fencing surrounding this can be seen in the right foreground of the 2001 photograph. Note how fashions have changed in 90 years! *Classic Pictures/CH*

LSWR CARRIAGE WORKS, EASTLEIGH: During the 1880s the London & South Western Railway decided to move its Carriage & Wagon Works from Nine Elms in London to Eastleigh. The new works were opened in 1891 situated to the east of the London-Southampton railway line at Barton, beside Bishopstoke Road. In 1909 the LSWR's Locomotive Works was also transferred from Nine Elms to Eastleigh, resulting in a considerable expansion of the railway works area to the south of the original Carriage & Wagon plant. Eastleigh became renowned as a railway town, and in public perception became linked with the LSWR in the same way as Swindon was linked with the Great Western Railway. Eastleigh's eminence continued through the Southern Railway period and for more than a decade into the nationalised era of British Railways. Change was to come as a result of Dr Beeching's plans to rationalise railway facilities in the 1960s. Production in the Locomotive Works ceased in 1965, although carriage repair and refurbishment was subsequently established in that part of the site.

Almost 100 years separate these views taken looking east from the bridge over the railway. The old Carriage & Wagon Works illustrated here was closed in 1968, and this area is now Barton Park Industrial Estate. Careful comparison of the two photographs shows that the buildings in the middle distance survive. After the closure of the Blenheim Road premises (see page 19), part of this site became Hants & Dorset's Eastleigh Depot in December 1976, with more of the area then being developed as Hants & Dorset's Central Repair Works as described on the following pages. With the break-up of Hants & Dorset in 1983 the Head Office of the Hampshire Bus Company was located here during that undertaking's period in public ownership, and part of the site still serves as Solent Blue Line's Eastleigh Depot, roofs of parked buses being glimpsed to the right of the bridge parapet in the 2001 photograph. *Classic Pictures/CH*

BARTON PARK: With the acquisition of the Trade Cars operation from Southampton Councillor S. Tebbutt in March 1920, Hants & Dorset gained some premises in Shirley Road, Southampton. This depot soon became the Company's engineering headquarters, and the interior of the body and paint shop can be seen in the first photograph, which dates from the mid-1920s. In 1935 premises were purchased in Winchester Road, Southampton, to supplement the by then cramped facilities at Shirley Road. Winchester Road became the Company's body and paint shop, but only hand painting (not spraying) could be done there.

The divided site was always a disadvantage, and by the mid-1970s there was an imperative need for more space.

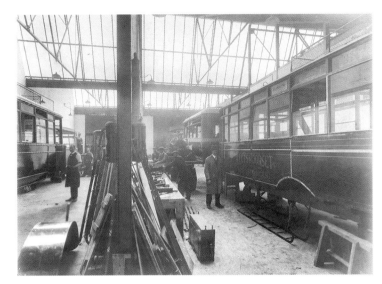

An area of 140,000 square feet was earmarked at the former railway carriage works at Barton Park, and following the transfer of Eastleigh Depot in 1976, a modern Central Repair works was established on the site, progressively brought into use over the following years. In the spring of 1977 Sir Frederick Wood, then Chairman of the National Bus Company, visited Hants & Dorset. Assistant Chief Engineer Rodney Luxton (now Chairman of the Wilts & Dorset Bus Company) can be seen showing Sir Frederick Wood a model of the proposed new facilities. Also in the photograph are (from the left) John Smith, Hants & Dorset Eastern Area Manager; Allan Rolls, Hants & Dorset Traffic Manager; Dawson Williams, Hants & Dorset Chief Engineer; Irwin Dalton, National Bus Company Regional Director, and Peter Hunt, Hants & Dorset General Manager.

The Hants & Dorset Central Repair Works at Barton Park were officially opened on 29 May 1981 by Sir David Price, MP for Eastleigh. A year later, on the first Saturday in June 1982 a public open day was held at Barton Park. Around 4,000 people visited and enjoyed a number of displays that detailed the wide variety of work carried out there. One of the attractions was a replica charabanc, seen here with cheerful passengers later that summer. This vehicle was originally a standard Bristol LH saloon, fleet number 3516 (NLJ 516M) new in October 1973 and withdrawn after serious accident damage in January 1980. Designed by Works Manager Reg Serpell and built at Barton Park, the charabanc carried a fleet number and registration once allocated to a 1920s Leyland saloon. Completed in May 1982 and resplendent in the old-style Hants & Dorset livery, this vehicle gave pleasure to many during the final months of that Company's existence. *Town & Country News/ Wilts & Dorset collection (2)*

BARTON PARK: Another Bristol LH, fleet number 1524 (REL 745H) new in August 1969, also underwent conversion work at Barton Park. One of the dual-doorway examples, the front section was fitted with a coffee machine and eight coach seats, arranged in two pairs facing each other across a table on each side. The rear section was fitted with tables and display boards for publicity, while a fin was fitted to the roof and used for posters. The resulting vehicle is seen in the spring of 1982, parked in Upper Market Street, Eastleigh, beside the old Railway Institute, which was built in 1891 and in its day provided many amenities both recreational and educational; sadly it was demolished during the 1980s and in 2001 a Safeway supermarket stands on the site. The publicity bus, as the vehicle became known, visited fetes, shows and exhibitions throughout 1982. I was working in the Company's publicity department at that time, and can be seen on the left in the second photograph, taken at Lee on Solent on a Sunday morning in June 1982. The other gentleman is Phil Coley, who had worked as a conductor at Hants & Dorset's Southampton Depot for a number of years; he was officially designated as a 'census-taker' following the end of crew operation, but he often helped at these events, where his great knowledge of the Eastern Area routes was most useful. Phil worked at Solent Blue Line's Head Office in Southampton until 2001, while REL 745H passed to Hampshire Bus in 1983. *Both Wilts & Dorset collection*

An earlier, and more extensive, conversion was carried out on Bristol Lodekka SRU 981, which was fitted out as a luxurious mobile restaurant; painted in Pullman livery, it was used by the Cotswold Hotel in Southampton. Later it was repurchased by Hants & Dorset Trim Ltd (see opposite), repainted in the old Hants & Dorset colours and used as a mobile hospitality unit. A well-stocked bar was fitted on the lower deck – this is the view looking towards the front bulkhead. SRU 981 was subsequently acquired by a purchaser in Kent; I saw it parked near Dymchurch in the summer of 2001, apparently disused. *Peter Drew*

BARTON PARK: In addition to acting as Hants & Dorset's Central Repair Works, the expertise available at Barton Park was marketed to other organisations, an 'Engineering Services' brochure being produced for this purpose. It is perhaps not generally known that bus companies do not themselves provide bus shelters; this is in fact a responsibility of local councils. One of the products offered for sale in the brochure was the 'Personcare Shelter', advertised as being of robust construction, using self-coloured glass reinforced polyester. The basic price (April 1981) was £294.00, plus an additional £20.00 for the optional seat as seen in this photograph of a newly completed shelter at Barton Park in 1981.

A number of local councils bought Personcare shelters for use at bus stops, and an example was photographed on the A31 near the junction of Oaks Drive at St Leonards on Friday 13 April 2001. Another example still in use in September 2001 was observed on Rownhams Lane, just to the north of the bridge over the M27 motorway.

With the break-up of Hants & Dorset in 1983, the works at Barton Park became a separate company called Hants & Dorset Engineering Ltd. In the new commercial climate the Company had to compete with other established and specialist undertakings, and unfortunately was soon forced to contract. Although Hants & Dorset Engineering Ltd closed down in January 1986, there is still some bus-related activity on the Barton Park site. As mentioned on page 24, Solent Blue Line's Eastleigh Depot is located in part of the premises, and the paint shop is now home to Hampshire Body & Paint, which as its name implies has been responsible for the repainting of many of the area's buses. Also initially established at Barton Park in 1986 was Hants & Dorset Trim Ltd, which specialises in the interior refurbishment of buses and coaches. This company has now moved to Northam, but in 2001 still keeps the old Hants & Dorset name alive. *Wilts & Dorset Collection/CH*

CRANBURY ROAD, EASTLEIGH: These photographs are looking north along Cranbury Road from its junction with Grantham Road. In the 'past' view, which dates from around 1910, All Saints' Mission Church can be seen on the street corner in the right foreground. This was built in 1891, and was used as a church hall after the present All Saints' Church on the corner of Desborough Road and Derby Road was consecrated in 1911. It eventually became a community centre known as Centre 66, but was burned down in June 1989. Eastleigh Borough Council provided a replacement building, which is further back from Cranbury Road and therefore out of view to the right of the 'present' photograph, taken on Saturday 23 June 2001. The new building is called the Cranbury Community Centre and was opened by the Mayor of Eastleigh on 16 December 1992; the foundation stone from the original Mission Church, dated 29 April 1891, is featured in the entrance foyer.

A group of youngsters stand in line for the photographer in the 1910 view – no doubt they were pupils at the school buildings seen behind them. The school building nearer to the camera was opened as Cranbury Road Infants School in 1891, and this building remains today; its external appearance is largely unchanged and 'Cranbury Road Infants School' is still in the stonework beneath the windows. It is now part of Eastleigh College. The building beyond it opened as a girls' school in 1893 but has been demolished and replaced by Maunsell House, as seen in the 2001 photograph; its name is a reminder of Eastleigh's railway past, for Richard Maunsell was Chief Mechanical Engineer of the Southern Railway from 1923 until 1937. Few external changes have been made to the terraced housing in the 91 years that separate the two photographs. *Classic Pictures/CH*

BISHOPSTOKE, RIVERSIDE: As a settlement Bishopstoke, or Stoke Episcopi, long predates Eastleigh, and, as its name suggests, it was once in the possession of the Bishop of Winchester. Until the later part of the 19th century Bishopstoke was largely an agricultural area, although there were a number of large houses for what might be termed 'the gentry'. When the railway first came to the area the present Eastleigh station was called Bishopstoke from 1841 until 1899 (see also page 20). After the relocation of the LSWR Carriage Works to Barton Park in 1891 (see page 24), houses were built for railway workers in Bishopstoke as well as in Eastleigh, and the area expanded. Nonetheless Bishopstoke remains a separate community, with a very pleasant atmosphere of its own.

The 'past' photograph dates from the 1920s and shows what was then called Mill Road running beside the River Itchen. Bishopstoke Mill can be seen in the right background; this has since been demolished and the road is now known as Riverside. When comparing the earlier scene with the 'present' photograph, taken on Monday 7 May 2001, it will be noticed that railings have been put up beside the river, and period-style street lighting has been provided in recent years. The buildings on the left have changed little. The Post Office remains, but the goods and services provided by the other shops have changed with the times. In the background the River Inn can be seen on the south side of Bishopstoke Road, opposite the junction with Riverside. This replaced a large house called St Agnes that formerly occupied the site and whose gates can be seen in the 'past' view. *Classic Pictures/CH*

FAIR OAK is situated just over 2 miles to the east of Eastleigh. Here we see Fair Oak Square, where the road from Eastleigh meets the road from Winchester to Botley. The importance of this junction is illustrated by the signpost in the 'past' photograph, which was taken around 1910. However, since the late 1970s the main road traffic to and from Eastleigh has been diverted along a new alignment to the south of Fair Oak Square, leaving the original road for local access (and buses) only. In earlier days the tree effectively formed something of a natural traffic island in the centre of the junction; by 2001 the pavement has been extended out to include the tree and the war memorial, erected after the First World War and inscribed to commemorate those lost in that conflict and in the 1939-45 war.

When the 'past' view was taken it seems that the local youngsters gathered to get themselves in the photograph; when I visited to take the 'present' picture during the early afternoon of Bank Holiday Monday 7 May 2001 the area was deserted. On the corner behind the tree used to be a typical village general store, selling all sorts of useful everyday things. These premises are now an Indian restaurant. Although the ground floor frontages of the terrace have been converted into shops, these outlets are not of the general store variety, but consist of a solicitor, a pine furniture showroom, an estate agent, a mortgage and insurance consultant (with pain relief clinic above) and a travel agent.

In the mid-1920s a company called Santoy Coaches started a bus service between Fair Oak and Eastleigh, competing with the Hants & Dorset service that had started in November 1920. Hants & Dorset purchased the goodwill of the Santoy route in June 1934 and it is effectively incorporated into the present-day Solent Blue Line service 48. *Classic Pictures/CH*

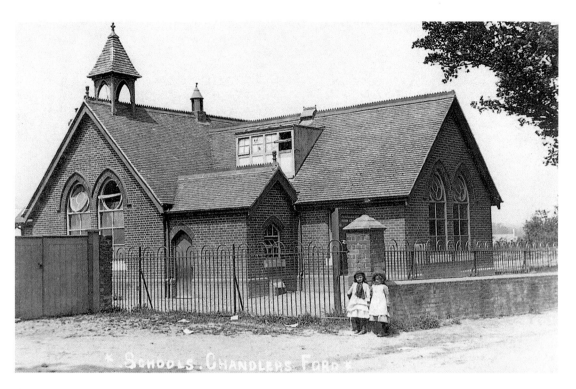

CHANDLER'S FORD SCHOOL: The first purpose-built school at Chandler's Ford opened in 1893, classes having previously been held in a church room. When opened the school catered for all children between 5 and 14, but by 1900 the buildings were already too small for the growing district. In 1908 a separate infants school was provided, with the children moving up to the 1893 premises for their education from the age of 9 until the then school leaving age of 14. The building ceased to be used as a school when North End Secondary Modern School opened in 1939. Shortly after the Second World War an engineering and plant hire business was started in the former school building by a Mr William Selwood. As this business expanded more extensive premises were needed, resulting in the demolition of the old school building in 1984. In 2001 only the fact that the road running along the north of the site is still called School Lane gives any indication that there was once a school here.

When the 'past' photograph was taken in the early 1900s two girls were happy to pose for the camera displaying the fashions of the era. On Saturday 8 September 2001 my god-daughters Saskia Wilkins (6) and Nikita Wilkins (5) came to Chandler's Ford with me to be photographed in the same location wearing modern clothes, almost 100 years on from the earlier view. *Classic Pictures/CH*

THE PARADE, CHANDLER'S FORD: The row of shops on the left, known as The Parade, was built during the 1930s on what was then known as Southampton Road (now called Bournemouth Road) in Chandler's Ford. In the 'past' photograph we see The Parade when newly built. Note the delightful ornate street lamps outside the shops. Sadly these had long vanished when the 'present' photograph was taken on Monday 7 May 2001, and while the row of shops is recognisable there seems to be an emphasis on ready-cooked food, with a balti house, pizza parlour and chip shop now among the outlets trading there.

The large advertisement seen in the 1930s view for the Bungalow Café in Southampton is interesting; road users going in the direction to see it would actually be travelling away from that City! Behind this advertisement a rather attractive building can be seen on the corner of Hursley Road. Originally built as a Post Office in 1900, by the 1930s it was used as offices by the Gas & Coke Company and later became an electrician's. It was demolished in 1984 to allow a roundabout to be built at this busy junction. Visible in the background to the left of the then Gas & Coke Company offices in the 'past' view is the Congregational Church in Kings Road, opened in October 1929; in recent years this structure has been extensively rebuilt, but cannot be seen in the 'present' photograph owing to the growth of trees in the intervening 65 or so years. *Classic Pictures/CH*

Winchester area

COLDEN COMMON is situated between Fair Oak and Winchester. When the 'past' photograph was taken around 1920 the building in the left foreground housed Clark's Stores and Colden Common Post Office. The 'present' view was taken on Monday 7 May 2001 and shows the unit nearest the camera as a beauty salon, while the centre unit was a specialist bowls supplier. The former Post Office is now a dental surgery, although this end of the building does carry a plaque recording its origins as 'The Old Post Office'. Notice how the brick-built pillar box has been replaced by a small pole-mounted version. Other buildings in the 'past' view can also be recognised in the 2001 photograph, and in general the scene is remarkably little changed.

The milk delivery cart, complete with churn, is of interest in the older view. At that time milk was decanted from the churn into customers' own containers. By the mid-1920s sales of pasteurised milk were increasing, delivered in wide-necked bottles sealed by cardboard lids. Milk bottles with foil tops were first introduced by United Dairies in 1935. Until the 1980s about 90 per cent of all milk used was delivered to the doorstep in glass bottles, but in 2001 only 25 per cent is delivered in this way, the remainder being bought mainly from supermarkets in either cardboard cartons or polythene bottles holding up to 6 pints. *Classic Pictures/CH*

SHAWFORD village lies between Compton and Twyford. In 2001 its public transport needs are met by Solent Blue Line Service 47, which stops near the junction of Otterbourne Road and Shawford Road (about 500 yards away), and by South West Trains – the railway station is just out of sight to the right of these photographs, taken in the late 1920s and on Monday 7 May 2001. However, Shawford was served by the King Alfred bus network from 1923 until that Company's route to Twyford was withdrawn in April 1969 – villagers made a farewell presentation to the crew of the final bus at the location shown here. Prior to this the railway bridge by the station had caused serious roof damage to double-deck buses in 1962 and 1963 – fortunately without casualties.

The Itchen Navigation, which also passes nearby, was once a freight route and barge horses used to be kept at the Bridge Hotel, seen on the left of the photographs. The Mission Hall dates from 1892 but sadly ceased to be used as such in 1956; building work was being undertaken in May 2001. In the 1920s the row of shops catered for the day-to-day needs of the village; in 2001 the businesses trading from the row were an architect, a beauty salon and an upholsterer offering 'quality hand-made three-piece suites'. The pillar box remains, but has been moved a few feet down the road. *Classic Pictures/CH*

TWYFORD, situated about 4 miles south of Winchester on the road to Botley, gained its name from two fords across the nearby River Itchen. When the 'past' photograph was taken around 1949 there was no traffic to be seen on the road. The picture shows a happy group of youngsters, and it is clearly quite safe for the two girls to stand in the roadway.

When I visited Twyford to take the 'present' photograph on Monday 7 May 2001 there were no pedestrians of any age to be seen, but there was a constant stream of traffic. It will be noticed that the crossroads is now controlled by traffic lights, while in the foreground a pelican crossing has been provided to help pedestrians cross this now busy road. A bus layby has been cut into the pavement, resulting in the replacement of the attractive wooden bus shelter with a more functional structure, just visible in the 'present' view. Twyford was served by Hants & Dorset buses from 1920 and King Alfred buses from 1923. The King Alfred service was withdrawn in April 1969, but the present-day services provided by Solent Blue Line and Stagecoach in Hampshire are descendants of the Hants & Dorset routes.

Twyford Post Office is still prominent on the left at the crossroads. This now also acts as a general stores and off-licence, and at the time of my visit a notice was displayed giving details of a planning application for an extension to provide tea-rooms and a tea garden. However, in the left foreground what was Hills & Sons' shop is now Twyford Antiques. *Classic Pictures/CH*

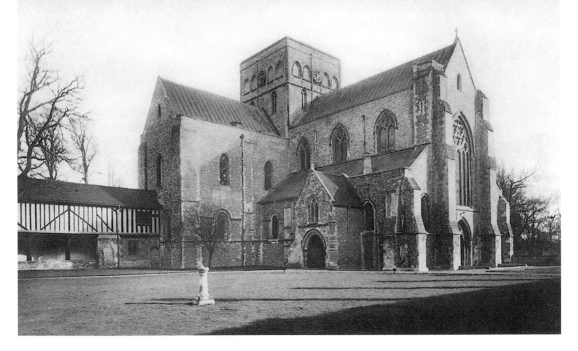

ST CROSS CHURCH, WINCHESTER, forms part of the Hospital of St Cross and the Almshouse of Noble Poverty. Building of the church commenced in 1135 when the Hospital was founded by the then Bishop of Winchester, Henry de Blois, and continued in stages for almost 200 years, with the North Porch, prominent in both photographs, being the final addition. The Hospital has provided a home for elderly men since the 12th century and is England's oldest such institution. The Almshouse of Noble Poverty was added in 1445 by another Bishop of Winchester, Cardinal Beaufort. This location continues to be a wonderfully peaceful living community in the 21st century. The elderly gentlemen who live here still wear the traditional gowns – black for the original Hospital foundation and red for the Almshouse of Noble Poverty. The residents say morning prayers each day in the church, and when a newcomer is admitted a short 'gowning' ceremony is held at this time. Another unique tradition that remains in 2001 is the Wayfarer's Dole of bread and ale, which is still given to travellers who request it at the Porter's Gate.

   Given the long history of the buildings, it is not surprising that apart from the trees there are virtually no changes apparent when comparing these photographs dating from the late 1940s and 2001; both illustrate the timeless charm and peace of the place. *Classic Pictures/CH*

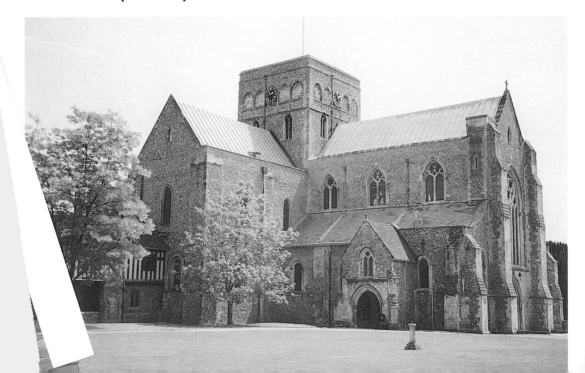

WINCHESTER HIGH STREET: We can date the 'past' photograph of Winchester High Street as having been taken in the early 1930s; the public house in the left foreground became the Talbot Hotel in 1929 (previously it had been the Star Inn) and a policeman wearing a white traffic coat can be seen on point duty at the staggered crossroads with Southgate Street and Jewry Street – traffic lights were installed here in 1934.

Although the location is easily recognisable in the 'present' photograph taken on Saturday 31 March 2001, a number of changes will be noted. The distinctive clock and the Buttercross can be seen in the background of both photographs; to the east of its junction with Jewry Street the High Street was pedestrianised in 1974 and crowds of Saturday afternoon shoppers can be seen in the 2001 view. The George Hotel, seen to the left of the policeman on the corner of Jewry Street, closed in 1939. It was demolished in 1956, and the Barclays Bank building, which can be seen on the site in the 'present' photograph, opened in 1959. The *Hampshire Observer*, which was produced at Warren's Printing Works on the left, ceased production in 1957. The erstwhile Talbot Hotel in the left foreground has been an estate agents for some years, but note that the brackets that formerly supported the public house signs remain! *Classic Pictures/CH*

THE SQUARE, WINCHESTER is situated to the south of the pedestrianised section of the High Street. The 'past' photograph was taken around 1959 and is a delightful period piece, epitomising the fashions and lifestyle of the time. The gentleman's bicycle has a dynamo hub on its front wheel, a feature popular at the time that provided power for the front and rear lights at night without the need for batteries. The problem was that the lights went out when you stopped! Nonetheless this form of lighting was legal for bicycles until the late 1960s. On the left deliveries are being made from a Morris Traveller, a classic design of vehicle of which a number are still on the road in 2001. Chalkey's traded from its corner position for more than 50 years; note the large fish sign projecting from the corner of the building, something of a local landmark from the early years of the 20th century.

Chalkey's closed in the early 1960s, and when the 'present' photograph was taken on 31 March 2001 a clothes shop called 'Little London' occupied the premises. The Square is still an attractive area, which today includes a wine bar and tea-rooms as well as traditional shops. Notice St Lawrence's Church, which can be seen in the background of both photographs.
British Travel Association (Wilts & Dorset collection)/CH

WINCHESTER CATHEDRAL: The first church to be built on this site dated from 648, and work began on the present building in 1079. Originally the priory of St Swithun, the building became known as Winchester Cathedral after the Dissolution. Despite various 'modifications' over the centuries, some Norman architecture remains, and the nave is the longest of any church in Europe. This magnificent church was found to be in danger of falling down in the early years of the 20th century; the water table is very close to the surface here, and a diver, one Mr William Walker, was employed between 1906 and 1911 to lay sacks of cement below the walls in order to underpin the foundations.

These photographs show the Cathedral in 1949 and on Saturday 31 March 2001. As would be expected, there have been few changes at this beautiful and historic location. The stonework of the building has been cleaned and new trees have been planted along the avenue on the left. Replica period street lamps have been provided, while in the foreground railings now mark the boundary with Great Minster Street. Notice how the trees on the right have grown in 52 years! *Etches & Co (Wilts & Dorset collection)/CH*

KINGSGATE, WINCHESTER, was an important part of the City's fortifications, and battlements are readily visible in both of these photographs, taken from the south of (ie outside) the wall. The first documented mention of the Kingsgate dates from 1148, and the structure is protected as an ancient monument. It is of particular interest in that its upper floor consists of the Church of St Swithun. Although churches over gates were fairly common in the Middle Ages, very few have survived, making St Swithun's a particularly rare and fine example. Entry to the church is via a staircase from the north side of the gate, and a visit to this beautiful little building where God has been worshipped for more than 700 years is highly recommended. Various 'restorations' have taken place over the years; the pitched roof seen behind the stone walls in the photographs is thought to date from the 17th century while the dormer windows just visible through the battlements were added during the 19th century to provide extra light. There is, nonetheless, a wonderful sense of history within the building.

The photographs were taken in 1949 and 2001, and as would be expected there have been relatively few changes during that 52 years. The wall and open area on the right replaced a house and shop demolished in the mid-1930s. It will be seen that the housing on the left has been replaced in more recent years; the replacement building is set further back from the road allowing more of the old city wall to be seen. Note that the rendering around the pavement arches, added during the 19th century, has been removed. Also missing from the 'present' photograph is the old-type road sign banning 'locomotives, motor tractors and heavy motor cars' from the Close. *Etches & Co (Wilts & Dorset collection)/CH*

THE BROADWAY, WINCHESTER: When Peter Trevaskis took the 'past' photograph from the Guildhall steps on 9 October 1965 he was able to include in the view the buses of three different operators. Coming towards the camera is Hants & Dorset fleet number 1451 (5678 EL), a Bristol FS6G new in 1961. This has a 60-seat rear-entrance body by Eastern Coach Works and is operating Service 47 from Southampton to Winchester. Going away from the camera on Service 14 to Aldershot is a Dennis Loline dating from 1958 with a 68-seat East Lancs body owned by Aldershot & District. And just visible through the tree behind the Rover car in the right foreground is 324 CAA, an AEC Bridgemaster with 74-seat rear-entrance bodywork by Park Royal; this was delivered new in July 1961 to King Alfred Motor Services, which at that time operated the City area routes. King Alfred Motor Services were taken over by Hants & Dorset in 1973 and the former Aldershot & District route is now part of the Stagecoach empire. Service 47 still runs regularly between Southampton and Winchester and is now operated by Solent Blue Line.

Changes to Winchester's road system have reduced the proportion of through traffic using the Broadway in the 36 years that separate the two photographs, and the alterations to the pavement at the pedestrian crossing in the foreground will be noted in the view taken from the same steps on 31 March 2001. Note the boys crossing the road on their micro-scooters while the bronze statue of King Alfred continues to keep an avuncular eye on the scene! *Aldershot & District Bus Interest Group/CH*

THE OLD CHESIL RECTORY was built in 1450 and is seen here in 1949 and 2001. Given the building's status as the oldest house in Winchester, it is not surprising that at first glance it has changed very little in the 52 years that separate the two photographs. However, close examination will show that there has been some rationalisation to the windows and chimney stacks, while the rather attractive wooden rail has been removed from the front of the building, which in fact was extensively refurbished in 1960-61. Note the sign on the wall on the right pointing the way to the Great Western Station – otherwise known as Winchester Chesil. Sharp eyes will notice that the word 'Great' has been painted out on the adjoining Private Road sign – an acknowledgement of nationalisation and the creation of British Railways the previous year. Winchester Chesil opened in May 1885 with the line south from Newbury, promoted by the Didcot, Newbury & Southampton Railway, but with train services provided from the outset by the GWR. The remaining link to the London & South Western Railway near Shawford was opened in January 1891.

Hidden away as it was, and with St Giles's Hill as a backdrop, Winchester Chesil had the atmosphere of a sleepy country station, in contrast to the purposeful bustle at Winchester City on the main line to London. In April 1950

the line to Newbury was transferred to the Southern Region, but patronage by then was already in steep decline. Closure to passengers in March 1960 was inevitable; the line continued to be used for freight for a few more years, but closed entirely in 1966. In 2001 a multi-storey car park stands on the site of the old station, and can be seen behind the Old Rectory in the modern photograph. However, by walking up the old station approach road it is still possible to see the (sealed) mouth of the tunnel that once took trains to Newbury beneath part of St Giles's Hill. *Etches & Co (Wilts & Dorset collection)/CH*

Romsey and Totton

ROMSEY ABBEY: The Abbey Church at Romsey was built on the site of an earlier Saxon church. It was constructed over a period of more than 100 years from 1120 onwards as part of a Benedictine nunnery, although a portion of the church was used for worship by the people of Romsey. The Dissolution and the eviction of the nuns left the residents of Romsey without a church, so £100 was raised to purchase the Abbey Church building, which in 1544 became Romsey's Parish Church.

The photographs are looking west along Church Place, around 1930 and on Saturday 7 April 2001, and, as would be expected, this magnificent Norman church has not changed in the interim. However, the demolition in the late 1950s of the buildings on the right of the 'past' photograph has given space for the pavement on the north side of Church Place to be widened and has enabled seats to be installed. On the opposite side of the road it will be noted that the wall from the gateway to the left-hand edge of the picture has been rebuilt on a new alignment, allowing that part of the roadway of Church Place to be moved slightly to the south. Note the handcart, three cars and the delightful charabanc in the 1930 picture; in 2001 cars occupy all the available on-street parking places. Romsey is a lovely town to look around on foot, and finger posts such as that seen in the foreground of the 'present' view now make such exploration easy for pedestrians. *Classic Pictures/CH*

ROMSEY TOWN CENTRE: These two photographs look from the east towards Romsey Market Place and the Abbey Church, and were taken in the early 1950s and on Saturday 7 April 2001. Although they are separated by a period of around 50 years, the general scene has changed little, although some detail differences can be observed. Study of the White Horse Hotel in the right foreground will confirm that the refurbishment of this building has involved some layout changes on the ground floor at least; like most of the former Trust House hotels it now comes under the Forte banner. W. H. Smith still occupies the same shop, but its corporate identity has been updated. The buildings at the end of this row are described opposite. In the left foreground what was Farmer's shoe shop is now an emporium entitled 'Age of Elegance'.

In the row of buildings in the background facing the camera the branch of Midland Bank has, like others, received the HSBC corporate identity, and a chemist still occupies the building on the right. However, between them what used to be The Cycle Works is now 'QD's Best Buy Far'. Romsey Abbey Church (see page 43) can be seen in the background with no visible exterior changes. Inside the church the present organ was originally installed in 1858; a Walker built to the design of F. A. Gore Ousely, it was extensively rebuilt by Walker in 1995-6, but fortunately care was taken to ensure that the original tonal quality was retained, and the instrument remains an excellent example of a Victorian church organ. Notice the changes in the parked vehicles and in the fashions worn by pedestrians! *Wilts & Dorset collection/CH*

The Old Swan Inn & Market Place, Romsey

ROMSEY MARKET PLACE: These photographs compare the scene looking northwards across Romsey Market Place towards the Church Street junction. The 'past' view dates from around 1900 while the present photograph was taken on Saturday 7 April 2001. Prominent in both photographs is the statue of Lord Palmerston, the Victorian Prime Minister famous for his 'gunboat diplomacy', who lived in nearby Broadlands House (open to the public at certain times, and well worth a visit) until his death in 1865. This statue, by Matthew Noble, was set up in the Market Place in 1868. A royal charter to hold a market in Romsey was granted in the 12th century; by the mid-19th century markets were held here each Thursday, but the Market Place ceased to be used for this purpose in 1919.

Behind Lord Palmerston's statue, what was Ely's ironmongery store is now a building society. The building next door and on the corner of Church Street is of considerable interest. The 'past' photograph bears a caption 'The Old Swan Inn', although the building itself is clearly titled 'Romsey Working Men's Conservative Association'. By 2001 the premises have been refurbished and no longer include Moore's printers and stationers, but a plaque beside the door confirms that this is still 'Romsey Working Men's Conservative Association'. It also records that the building stands on the site of the old Swan Inn, one of the oldest licensed premises in Romsey. The plaque goes on to relate, 'It is recorded that in 1642 two soldiers from Cromwell's Army were hanged from the wrought iron sign bracket on this wall'. *Classic Pictures/CH*

ROMSEY STATION was opened in 1847 with the line from Bishopstoke (Eastleigh) to Salisbury. When the line from Southampton to Andover was opened in 1865 Romsey became a pivotal station for four routes. The 'past' view dates from around 1910 and shows a number of the station staff on the platform used by trains bound for Eastleigh or Southampton. The line to Andover was closed in September 1964 and regular passenger services were withdrawn from the line to Eastleigh in May 1969. However, this latter route remained open for freight, and in recent years a few passenger trains have also been scheduled to use the line.

Romsey is still a well-used station in 2001, with the majority of its train services running between Portsmouth and Bristol or South Wales; appropriately the station now sports Wales & West corporate identity. The 'present' photograph was taken on Saturday 7 April 2001, and it is pleasing to note that much remains little changed from the older view. The protection for the subway on the left was rebuilt in the early 1960s, while the sidings behind the platform were taken out of use in the 1970s. The loss of the water column for steam locomotives and the installation of colour light signalling will be noted. Note also the addition of a covered storage area for bicycles in the right foreground. *Classic Pictures/CH*

Nutshalling (Nursling) Church.

NURSLING: Since the 1970s the community of Nursling has been bisected by the M27 motorway. The church, dedicated to St Boniface, is easily seen from the motorway, but I suspect that few who hurry along that highway have ventured down the narrow dead-end lane to look at it more closely. That is a pity, because this seemingly insignificant spot is in fact of considerable interest. In the 7th century there was an important Christian community here that had links with nearby Romsey, and Nursling was regarded as a centre of learning and prayer. St Boniface, born in Devon in 680, came from the Benedictine Abbey of Exeter to Nursling to teach. He later travelled Europe as a Christian missionary, and his ministry led to the conversion of many, especially in Germany. The church building seen in these photographs is mostly 14th century, but was 'restored' in the 19th century. The building is more visible in the 'past' photograph, which dates from around 1920; the large bushes in the right foreground obscure part of the building in the 'present' view, taken on Saturday 7 April 2001. However, as would be expected, there have been few changes to the outside of the church building in the 80 or so years which separate the two photographs.

The large horse chestnut tree that dominates the 'past' view, and which no doubt kept the youngsters pictured well supplied with conkers, was cut down in the late 1970s. The old-style street lamp has gone, and has not been replaced by a modern equivalent. Behind the high wall on the left of the photographs is the former rectory, which dates from 1788. Looking at the tranquil scene in the 'present' view, it is hard to believe that the hectic M27 is so close by. *Classic Pictures/CH*

CALMORE has a history dating back to the Iron Age when a hill fort was built at Tatchbury Mount, about 800 yards to the west of these photographs as the crow flies, where in 2001 there is a large psychiatric hospital. The photographs are looking north along Calmore Road, and were taken around 1930 and on Easter Monday, 16 April 2001. Calmore has seen considerable expansion from the 1950s onwards, and it is pleasing to see how the new development has been fitted in around the existing buildings. Calmore Post Office continues to thrive, and additionally is now a very useful local store. Customers entering the newer part of the building can walk through into the ground floor of the original post office building, so there has been a large expansion in the amount of retail space, mirroring the enlargement of the local community. The front garden of the original post office has gone, as has the attractive glazed porch and indeed the front door – note the modern-type pillar box below the lintel of the bricked-up former entrance.

Construction of the new section of the building has required the removal of the trees seen in the centre of the 1930 photograph. However, this does open up a better view of the next house, which can be recognised from its porch seen in the earlier view. It can be seen how bungalows occupy what was previously open country beyond, while the made-up road, complete with kerbs and pavements, gives the area a distinctly suburban feel. Nonetheless it is possible on foot to be out in the country in minutes from here, and the area remains a very pleasant one. *Classic Pictures/CH*

TOTTON STATION: The railway line between Southampton and Dorchester via Brockenhurst and Ringwood was opened as a single track in 1847, but the main buildings of Totton station date from 1859 when the line was doubled, and can be seen on the 'up' platform in both of these photographs. The views are taken looking westwards from the station footbridge, and date from 1910 and Saturday 24 March 2001. It can be seen that the main building survives with few changes to its appearance, although the wooden building immediately beyond it – at one time the Station Master's office – has gone. However, all of the buildings have been removed from the 'down' platform and replaced by a very basic shelter. The line was electrified in July 1967 and in recent years there has been an increase in the number of trains stopping at Totton, with both slow and semi-fast services now calling here. *Classic Pictures/CH*

STATION ROAD, TOTTON: Totton is mentioned in the Domesday Book, but for centuries was overshadowed in importance by neighbouring Eling. From the mid-19th century onwards, however, Totton has grown rapidly and continues to grow, while Eling has become a quiet backwater. These photographs compare Station Road around 1910 and on Saturday 24 March 2001. The Station Hotel seen on the left was tied to Ashby's Eling Brewery in 1910. Eling Brewery was founded in 1824 and acquired by Francis Ashby in 1857; Ashby's was taken over by Strong's of Romsey in 1921, and beer ceased to be brewed at Eling. In 2001 the Station Hotel is a free house, but there have been few changes to its external appearance.

In the 1910 view the Red Lion public house can be seen in the background beyond the level crossing. In 1930 this level crossing was closed, together with the signal box visible on the right of the 'past' view. Pedestrians can still cross the railway here by means of the footbridge, which also serves as the station footbridge and is completely unchanged in appearance. In the background the Red Lion has been extensively modernised, although the wall beside the railway now obscures much of the view of the building from this point. The terrace on the right of Station Road beyond the railway line survives, but the ground floors are no longer in retail use.
Classic Pictures/CH

The Waterside

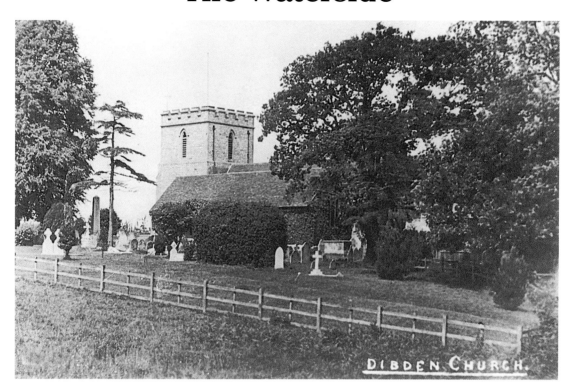

ALL SAINTS' CHURCH, DIBDEN, dates originally from the 13th century, its list of rectors going back to 1262. Various additions and 'restorations' have taken place, notably during the 19th century, when the present tower was erected in 1882-4. During the early hours of Thursday 20 June 1940 the church achieved the dubious distinction of becoming the first in the British Isles to be destroyed in the Second World War, being gutted by incendiary bombs. It was restored in 1955 to a simpler but very attractive design, the new nave walls being built with stone recovered from the former building. The change in the exterior appearance of the church can be seen by comparing these photographs, taken prior to the war and on 16 April 2001. Inside the church the 13th-century chancel arch survives, and the font, which was damaged in 1940, has been repaired and repositioned. The rebuilt organ is the work of Bishop & Son. *Classic Pictures/CH*

WEST STREET, HYTHE: It is difficult to believe that these two photographs, taken around 1920 and on Monday 16 April 2001, show the same location. The transformation of the scene commenced in the 1960s when material dredged from Millbrook on the other side of Southampton Water during the building of the container terminal was dumped here, so reclaiming a considerable area. In 1984 work started to develop this reclaimed area as Hythe Marina Village, incorporating more than 200 homes, with local shops in a 'neighbourhood centre' as well as the usual facilities for boats. Hythe Marina is now an established and attractive area, and is located to the left of the 2001 photograph. By looking carefully it is just possible to discern in the modern view the line of the bank on the right of the 1920 picture. Given that high tides once lapped almost up to this bank, it is clear that our modern engineers have had more success than King Canute in restraining the sea in this area! *Classic Pictures/CH*

HYTHE PIER is 700 yards long and was built during 1879-80, being officially opened on 1 January 1881. The Hythe Pier Railway opened to passengers in July 1922, and replaced a tramway provided to convey luggage on hand-propelled trolleys from 1909. Locomotives for the 2-foot-gauge trains were bought second-hand from the Avonmouth Mustard Gas Factory, for whom they had been built by Brush of Loughborough in 1917 to run on 100-volt batteries. For use on Hythe Pier they were adapted for third-rail operation at 200 volts, their traction batteries being removed. Passenger carriages for the trains were built by the Drewry Car Company Limited.

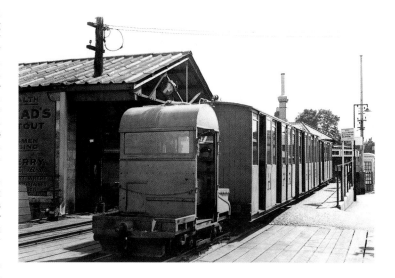

The 'past' photograph shows the train at the landward end of Hythe Pier on 25 June 1933, with the locomotive at the sea end of the train. Note the telephone kiosk to the right of the rear of the train; this is built in concrete and is of the K3 design first introduced in 1929. The GPO provided around 12,000 telephone kiosks of this design in various parts of the country between 1929 and 1935.

The 'present' photograph was taken on Tuesday 22 May 2001. The train is in the same position as 68 years previously, but the locomotive is now at the shore end of the train, giving a view of the control trailer carriage. The addition of a sheltered area on the right of the train will be noted, but the building on the left is still readily identifiable. The line is still worked by the same locomotives and stock that opened the service in 1922, and is now advertised as the oldest working electric pier train in the world.

Originally the carriages were painted green with the letters 'HPR' in cream on the sides. For some years the trains have run in a red and white colour scheme, but for the 2001 season one of the carriages was restored to its original livery, as can be seen in the third photograph, also taken on 22 May 2001. *White Horse Ferries/CH (2)*

NEW ROAD, HYTHE: Until the late 19th century Hythe was not a parish in its own right, but was included in the Parish of Fawley. In 1823 a daughter church of All Saints' Fawley was built in Hythe and dedicated to St John. This was replaced in 1874 when Hythe became a separate parish by the present St John's Church, designed by John Oldrid Scott and seen on the right of both these photographs, which date from around 1950 and 2001. The scene is quite recognisable – even the pine trees in the foreground survive.

It will be noted that the old hall opposite the church has been replaced by a modern brick building. A foundation stone for this was laid on 10 March 1998 by the Bishop of Southampton, Rt Rev Jonathan Gledhill, and the building is dedicated 'for our children'. Behind the new church hall the flat-roofed 1960s building blends in less well. Notice the traffic-calming measure, which also forms a crossing place between the church and the hall. *Classic Pictures/CH*

DIBDEN PURLIEU is situated just west of Hythe on the road towards Beaulieu. These photographs show the junction of Beaulieu Road and North Road in the late 1940s and in 2001. In the 1940s the corner shop was operated by Frank Blunden, and served as Dibden Purlieu's post office (note the pillar box and stamp machines outside), grocery and dairy. The 1960s replacement building incorporates an equally useful local shop providing Dibden Purlieu with a newsagent, grocer and off-licence as well as its post office. The building in the centre of the photographs is readily identifiable in both views, and proves that they were taken from the same location. The traditional bench seat has been replaced by some rather stylish modern street furniture, which provides comfortable seating for a much larger number of people. *Classic Pictures/CH*

HARDLEY: This school at Hardley was in use from 1871 until 1925. The early years of the school would appear to have been rather turbulent, with frequent changes of staff between 1884 and 1890, including one schoolmistress who resigned owing to nervous strain, feeling unequal to teaching. HM Inspector of Schools considered the situation unsatisfactory, despite having made allowance for what it termed 'special difficulties'. However, with the appointment of a new schoolmistress in October 1890 matters at the school, which was categorised as being for girls and infants, quickly improved, and by May 1891 HMI was able to praise the standards of teaching. The 1890s were a halcyon period for the school, with consistently excellent HMI reports and with new desks and other equipment being provided following recommendations in the 1897 report. However, problems resurfaced at the turn of the century, with another period of high staff turnover. The HMI reports of this time comment on the decline in standards at the school, and matters came to a head in June 1906 when the managers decided to close the school after 'some unpleasantness' resulting in the then schoolmistress terminating her employment. The school re-opened in September 1906, and by October 1908 HMI was pleased to comment that, in contrast to the rather unfavourable report three years previously, the school was now 'in excellent order'. The 'past' photograph seen here dates from 1909 and shows the pupils by the north side of the building.

The school closed in 1925 but the building remains in residential use as seen in the 'present' photograph, taken on Monday 16 April 2001; it is now adjoined by a housing development called Old School Close, which required the 'present' photograph to be taken from a slightly different location when compared with the 1909 view. The present very successful Hardley School in Long Lane dates from 1935, following the expansion of housing in the area from the early 1930s. *Classic Pictures/CH*

FAWLEY is mentioned in the Domesday Book, but is probably best known for its huge oil refinery, originally opened on a smaller scale by the Anglo, Gulf, West Indies Petroleum Corporation in the early 1920s. This was expanded into a huge complex by Esso after the Second World War; the new refinery occupies almost 2 miles of shoreline and was opened by Clement Attlee in 1951.

The photographs show Fawley Square in the early 1930s and on Tuesday 22 May 2001, and the scene is readily recognisable. The Falcon Hotel on the right dates from the mid-19th century and is little changed. The shop next door also retains a similar appearance, but whereas in the 1930s this was a sweet shop called The Chocolate Box, in 2001 the premises were home to a florist. The large house in the centre of the photographs dates back to the 17th century and was originally the Blue Anchor Inn. In both of these photographs it is a private residence; notice how the porch has been modified and the chimneys removed in the 70 or so years which separate the two views – in 2001 the building sports the name 'Blue Anchor House'. R. J. Light's shop was built in the 1920s and sold boots and shoes; in the 1950s it was Gray's radio and electrical store, but nowadays caters for a section of the local leisure market as 'Specialised Sailing'. Just visible on the left of both photographs is part of the Jubilee Hall, built in 1887 to mark 50 years of Queen Victoria's reign. *Classic Pictures/CH*

BLACKFIELD is located on the eastern edge of the New Forest, on the road leading to Lepe Beach. These photographs compare the scene at Blackfield Cross Roads, looking north along Hampton Lane, in the late 1930s and in 2001. The area still had a very rural look in the 1930s, but a regular bus link to Southampton had been established by that time. The large notice beside the gates of Shelley's off-licence on the Exbury Road is a timetable case for the Hants & Dorset bus route; the smaller notice beside it indicates that the off-licence also acted as a parcel agent for the bus company.

The house in the centre of the 'past' photograph is also seen in the modern view, and fixes the location. The scene has changed considerably, with much new building apparent and road layout changes to take into account the increased flow of traffic. A passenger is seen waiting for a Solent Blue Line bus to Southampton in the bus shelter by the flat-roofed shopping parade as storm clouds gather in the late afternoon of Monday 16 April 2001. Also apparent in the modern photograph are high-voltage electricity lines linking the power station at nearby Fawley with the National Grid. *Classic Pictures/CH*

EXBURY qualifies for inclusion in our exploration as it has a Solent Blue Line bus service on summer Sundays to serve the renowned Exbury Gardens, a wonderful collection of rhododendrons and other beautiful plants laid out by Lionel de Rothschild in the 1920s. Exbury House was requisitioned by the Admiralty during the Second World War and not handed back until 1955, but the grounds have been expertly restored and are open to the public in season – a visit when the bushes are at their best is highly recommended.

These photographs, taken in the late 1950s and on 16 April 2001, show Exbury's village shop and post office. This was built in the 1930s and replaced an earlier shop on the same site that dated from around 1860. Sadly the village shop and post office closed in 1987 and the building is now used throughout as residential accommodation, although its outward appearance is little changed. Notice the old-style telephone sign attached to the telegraph pole in the 1950s photograph; the telephone kiosk itself can just be seen over the top of the hedge on the shop forecourt, but this has also now been removed. *Classic Pictures/CH*

Woolston, Netley and Hamble

WOOLSTON FLOATING BRIDGE/ITCHEN BRIDGE: Records of a ferry service across the River Itchen between Southampton and Woolston go back to at least the 16th century, the service being operated by the fishermen of Woolston. In 1833 the Itchen Bridge Company was formed with the intention of building a swing bridge here, but this proposal was vetoed by the Admiralty. Therefore a steam-powered floating bridge was provided instead, and operations commenced on 23 November 1836. The 'past' photograph dates from around 1904 and shows bridge No 7 on the Woolston side of the crossing. Built in 1892 by Summers at Northam (see also page 17) this particular craft came to an ignominious end on 8 March 1928 when it was struck by a tug in mid-crossing, broke from its cables and sank almost 200 yards downstream. As this happened in the late afternoon there were many people on the bridge at the time, but fortunately all were rescued without casualties. The Company was purchased by Southampton Corporation in 1934, and tolls for pedestrians and cyclists were abolished in 1946, although charges for vehicles were retained.

As early as 1936 the Corporation had considered plans to replace the floating bridges with a fixed bridge or even a tunnel, but proposals were shelved with the approach of the Second World War. Discussions about a possible bridge recommenced in 1955, but it was not until March 1974 that work started on the bridge, which opened to traffic in June 1977. The last public crossing of the floating bridge took place at 11pm on Saturday 11 June 1977. Twenty-four years later the Itchen Bridge is part of the landscape, and its graceful spans were photographed during the early evening of Saturday 12 May 2001 from the same location as the 'past' picture.
Classic Pictures/CH

OBELISK ROAD, WOOLSTON: In 1855 a Mr Lankester opened a post office, off-licence and grocery shop in Obelisk Road, Woolston. The business thrived and in 1880 Mr Lankester was joined by a Mr Spencer, and as Lankester & Spencer the undertaking grew, with another branch being opened in Victoria Road, Woolston, followed by others in Bitterne, Netley and Titchfield. Following the retirement of Mr Spencer in 1890, Mr Lankester was joined by Mr S. B. Crook, bringing into being the still well-remembered title 'Lankester & Crook (County Supply Stores)'. Further expansion followed, and by 1963 the Company had 15 shops controlled from its Head Office at the original Obelisk Road premises, which had been extended in 1891 as a department store. As well as groceries and a butchery, departments included medicines, stationery and fancy goods, pet foods, corn and seeds, furnishing, general ironmongery, and china, glass and earthenware. A particular favourite was 'Obelisk' coffee, specially blended for the water of the district.

These photographs show the Obelisk Road building around 1920 and on Saturday 12 May 2001. Lankester & Crook pulled out of the retail trade in 1986, and when the 'present' view was taken the building looked superficially similar but had been divided into five units, that nearest the camera being a dance-wear shop, followed by a printer and a plumber, the two furthest units being vacant. *Classic Pictures/CH*

ABBEY HILL, NETLEY: The coast road from Woolston to Netley takes a pleasant course via Weston Shore and Abbey Hill. When the 'past' photograph was taken around 1960, Hants & Dorset fleet number 1029 (JT 9357) was operating a Service 81 journey between Woolston and Hamble via Netley. This Bristol K5G was placed in service in July 1938, and in June 1949 was fitted with a new 55-seat Eastern Coach Works lowbridge body; the front destination equipment was modified to the layout seen here in June 1959. JT 9357 was withdrawn in September 1964.

The same spot was photographed on Saturday 26 May 2001. The fence on the seaward side of the road has been replaced, but in general time has stood still at this attractive location. However, it has been many years since the characteristic growl of the five-cylinder Gardner engine in a Bristol K5G has been heard climbing the hill! *Wilts & Dorset collection/CH*

NETLEY ABBEY was established in 1239 by Cistercian monks from Beaulieu and was built with the support of King Henry III. With the Dissolution the Abbey was granted to Sir William Paulet in 1536, who converted part of the building into a house, which was occupied until 1700. After this some of the stonework was sold for use as building material elsewhere, but the story runs that demolition was halted when those involved started to suffer terrifying nightmares, which chillingly came true when a workman was killed by a stone window surround falling on him.

The Abbey ruins have been an attraction for visitors since the mid-18th century. The photographs, dating from around 1910 and Saturday 26 May 2001, are taken from the Nave looking east across the Quire. The ruins passed into the hands of the Ministry of Works in 1922, and are now in the care of English Heritage. Still a tourist attraction with free access, the removal of the ivy from the walls is a visual improvement as well as helping the conservation of the ruins. As expected, the view itself is substantially little changed in the 90 years that separate the two photographs, but the better care taken of the site in 2001 is noticeable. *Classic Pictures/CH*

STATION ROAD, NETLEY: Although the Abbey from which it takes its name dates from 1239, much of the settlement of Netley as we know it today was developed from the mid-19th century onwards, following the construction of the Royal Victoria Hospital and the arrival of the railway. Station Road is shown on a map dated 1870, but the buildings in the section of road illustrated here are from a slightly later date. The photographs compare the view looking north along Station Road from its crossroads with New Road in the early 1950s and on Saturday 26 May 2001. Prominent in the right foreground of the 'past' photograph is Lankester & Crook's County Supply Stores (see also page 61), complete with an attractive canopy. In 2001 most of this shop is a branch of Alldays and is therefore still a useful source of provisions for the local community. Note the wall-mounted cash machine for the Royal Bank of Scotland, which is prominently signed. The far end of the former Lankester & Crook emporium is now the Hound Parish Council Office, while the large building beyond is still Netley Central Sports & Social Club.

In the 1950s view a Morris 1000 van, a type much associated with the GPO, is standing outside the post office; Netley Post Office is still located in the same premises in 2001. What was a men's and boys' outfitters in the left foreground is now a branch of Lloyds/TSB, while on the other side of the crossroads the garage has been replaced by housing in recent years. The bus stop remains in the same place; the once familiar green and cream Hants & Dorset pole and flag can be seen on the left of Station Road in the 'past' photograph, while a functional but stylish shelter has been provided by 2001. The guard rails at the crossroads, the increase in traffic and the heritage-style street lighting will all be noted in the 2001 photograph. *Classic Pictures/CH*

NETLEY STATION: In 1866 a single-track branch railway was opened from St Denys to Netley, where the line terminated until 1889 when a single track onwards to Fareham was opened. The track between St Denys and Netley was doubled in 1910, with the continuation to Fareham following in 1911. These photographs were taken looking towards St Denys, and compare the station around 1920 and on Saturday 26 May 2001. The scene is easily recognisable after a gap of more than 80 years; both the main building on platform 1 and the smaller building on platform 2 survive largely unaltered. After semaphore signalling was replaced by colour lights in 1980, the signal box was removed from platform 1, finding a new home at Ropley on the preserved Mid-Hants Railway. Steam trains were replaced on most journeys by diesel multiple units in 1957 and the line was electrified in May 1990. Modern platform lighting, seats and South West Trains corporate identity signs have all been installed in recent years, and the station is still well used in 2001. *Classic Pictures/CH*

THE ROYAL VICTORIA HOSPITAL, NETLEY, was the first hospital to be purpose built for the British Army. In 1855 Queen Victoria had seen for herself the appalling conditions under which invalid soldiers returning from the Crimean War were being looked after, and she put pressure on the Government to take immediate steps to improve the situation. The site at Netley was purchased in January 1856, and the Queen herself laid a foundation stone for the building on 19 May of that year. The hospital building was 468 yards long, with some internal corridors extending for nearly a quarter of a mile. Presumably to give an impressive façade when viewed from the sea, the hospital was built with the corridors facing Southampton Water while the wards faced north-east and looked out on to gloomy courtyards. Florence Nightingale, returned from the Crimean War base hospital at Scutari, was horrified and attempted to get the plans altered, but to no avail, and the massive building was opened in March 1863. A separate annex, used as an asylum, was opened in 1870, becoming Britain's first purpose-built military asylum. For a time the hospital was very well used, and indeed during the First World War its capacity was almost doubled by the establishment of a Red Cross hutted hospital behind the main building. It was again filled to capacity during the Second World War and for a time was used by the American forces, who drove jeeps down the long, wide corridors.

During the 1950s the main building gradually fell into disuse, and in 1963 the central block was severely damaged by fire. In 1966 all of the main building apart from the chapel was demolished; these photographs show the west wing of the hospital in its heyday and, taken from the same point, the remaining chapel on 26 May 2001.
Lingwood Netley Hospital Archive/CH

THE ROYAL VICTORIA HOSPITAL, NETLEY: This photograph, dating from the early years of the 20th century, gives a better impression of the massive size of the hospital; well under half of the building is visible in the 'past' view opposite. The 'present' photograph, taken from the same position on Saturday 26 May 2001, gives a good view of the chapel in which both Queen Victoria and Florence Nightingale are said to have worshipped.

Although the chapel was all that remained of the main building after 1966, the asylum annex continued in use until 1979, when the Army finally vacated the site. The former asylum is now a police training college. Hampshire County Council purchased the main site when the Army left, and opened it to the public as the Royal Victoria Country Park in May 1980. The chapel is now used as a visitor centre and for exhibitions, and unfortunately most of the original interior furnishings have long been removed. One treasure remains, however – the organ, a Bevington dating from 1855. Apart from routine tuning and maintenance, very little work has been done on this instrument, which therefore remains an excellent example of the sound of a chapel organ of the Victorian era. I would love to arrange a hymn-singing session here, choosing from Ancient & Modern (Standard Edition, of course!) hymns with lovely old tunes by J. B. Dykes, Joseph Barnby, John Stainer, F. A. Gore Ousely, Arthur Sullivan and others, all sung in traditional four-part harmony and accompanied by that fine organ. *Lingwood Netley Hospital Archive/CH*

THE ROYAL VICTORIA HOSPITAL, NETLEY: I am told by a friend who has retired from a distinguished and respected career in the National Health Service that most hospitals accommodated in old buildings are reputed to be haunted – the 'ghost' often taking the form of a 'grey lady'. The Royal Victoria Hospital was no exception, and a number of accounts exist of a ghostly 'grey lady' being seen, said to be the ghost of a nurse who had committed suicide in the early days of the hospital, and the spectre was regarded by some as a harbinger of death. On 31 October 1966 (Hallowe'en), with the demolition of the main building imminent, a 'ghost hunt' was undertaken with the permission (and therefore the knowledge) of the contractor. I suspect that the latter decided to ensure that his guests were appropriately entertained, for they apparently saw from some distance a figure wearing an old-style nurse's uniform. To make sure that they did not miss the performance, the arrival of the 'ghost' was announced by a note being played on an old broken piano near the point of the 'phantom's' appearance!

Interestingly enough, stories still emerge of ghostly goings-on, both in the Country Park and at the nearby military cemetery, and some people claim that there is an 'atmosphere' in parts of the site. All I can say is that while I acknowledge that great pain and suffering was endured here when the hospital cared for injured servicemen years ago, during visits to the Country Park over a number of years I have never felt any sense of disquiet here. Our last photographs of the site compare patients walking in the hospital grounds with the same location as part of the Royal Victoria Country Park on Saturday 26 May 2001. *Lingwood Netley Hospital Archive/CH*

HAMBLE: The use of the name Hamble goes back to at least the 8th century, when the area's double tides were noted by the Venerable Bede. The full title of the village is Hamble le Rice, probably derived from the Norman French 'en le rys', meaning that the village was on a small hill. For many years Hamble has been associated with maritime activities, as can be seen in the background of both of these photographs, which look towards Hamble Quay. A number of young people, probably wearing their best clothes and posing for the camera, can be seen in the 'past' photograph, which dates from 1905. In the 'present' view we can see the more informal modern fashions as people enjoy the early evening sunshine on Saturday 26 May 2001.

The Bugle Inn can be seen on the right of both photographs. Parts of this building are over 800 years old, and it certainly occupies an idyllic location. It will be noted how the building has been modernised in the 96 years separating the two photographs, but the flight of steps up to the door, prominent in the 1905 view, still exists and part of the handrail can just be seen in the 2001 photograph. The four cottages seen in the left background of the 'past' photograph are still there, but are now hidden by the large tree. Originally dating from 1819, the row is now occupied by the Royal Southern Yacht Club. Before the Second World War most of the foreshore in the Quay area was mud, but during the war the American forces reclaimed the muddy area so that it could be used to maintain landing-craft. Some of this reclaimed land can be seen in the 2001 view; people can now sit and watch the peaceful activities on the river. Fame of sorts came to the area in 1986 when the BBC television series *Howards' Way* was set in nearby Bursledon (renamed 'Tarrant' for the programme). Some scenes were filmed in Hamble, and the popularity of the series brought many extra tourists to the area. *Classic Pictures/CH*

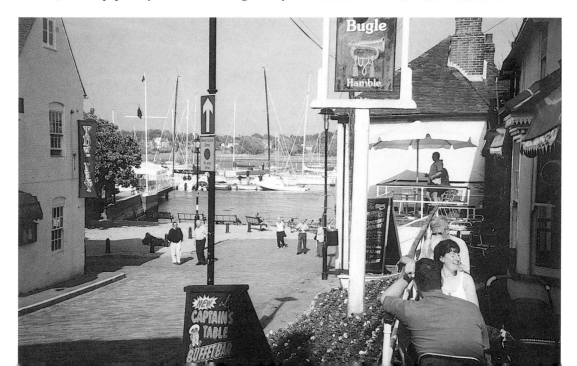

Hedge End, Botley and the Meon Valley area

HEDGE END is situated between Southampton and Botley, and early references to the name date back to the 18th century, when the district consisted simply of a number of farms and smallholdings. By the early 19th century the village of Hedge End was becoming established, and development has continued thereafter, with large housing areas being built in the latter part of the 20th century, and, following the completion of the M27 motorway, a complex of superstores. During the 1860s the Warner family of Botley, who owned much of the land then being developed, made available an area beside St John's Road for use as a recreation ground. At first Mr Warner remained responsible for its upkeep, but it was taken over by the Parish Council in 1895.

In the 'past' photograph, taken around 1922, we see part of the recreation ground looking north along St John's Road. Just visible in the background immediately to the right of the tree is the gable end of the National School, opened in January 1864, closed in July 1984 and now used as a youth and community centre. In the 2001

photograph the view of the former school is blocked by the modern police station building, to the right of which can be seen part of the village hall, originally opened in 1962 and later extended. The houses on the left of St John's Road remain; in the background the Fountain public house has been rebuilt, but remains on the same site. Beyond the Fountain in the 'past' view the former Bible Christian Chapel is just visible; built in 1865, it became a Methodist Chapel in 1907 and was replaced in 1924 by a new building further along St John's Road. Remarkably, some of the recreation ground fencing seems to have survived through the years!
Classic Pictures/CH

HEDGE END TOLL GATE: In 1799-1800 a turnpike road was built by the Northam Bridge Company from Southampton to Botley. The Company collected tolls to pay for the upkeep of the bridge and the road, with toll gates at several points along the way. One such collection point was located on what is still called Lower Northam Road at Hedge End, and is seen in the 'past' photograph during the 1920s. The view is looking towards Botley, and the toll collector lived in the cottage to the left of the toll bar in what was then a relatively isolated situation.

The road between Southampton and Botley was made free on 16 May 1929. The Mayor of Southampton, Councillor Maurice Pugh, proceeded along the road to Botley, ceremonially freeing the toll gates during the course of his journey. A touch of farce was added to the proceedings here at Hedge End as the toll bar had been stolen by some local lads during the previous night, resulting in improvised arrangements having to be made for the ceremony!

The same location is seen in the 'present' photograph, taken on Saturday 19 May 2001. It is easy to imagine the chaos that would ensue if the traffic now using the road had to stop at a toll gate. The scene now has a much more suburban and built-up appearance, and at first glance nothing can be seen to remind us of the 'past' view. However, the bench seen in the foreground marks the site of the former toll gate; it was presented in 1979 to commemorate the freeing of the toll road 50 years previously. *Classic Pictures/CH*

BOTLEY is an attractive village at the highest point to which tides flow on the River Hamble. Until the early part of the last century it was a small port; colliery boats came up the river to Botley until 1920, and it is said that local people would trawl the river after unloading to glean the spilt coal. The 19th-century writer William Cobbett, known for his *Rural Rides*, lived in Botley between 1804 and 1817, which he described as 'delightful'.

These photographs compare Botley Square in the early 1950s and on Saturday 19 May 2001. At one time a staging post on the coaching routes, Botley still has a number of inns, one of which, the Bugle, is seen towards the right of these photographs. In the 1950s the Bugle was tied to Strong's of Romsey, a thriving brewery that had advertisements all over Hampshire declaring 'You're in the Strong Country'. The demise of this locally famous name came in 1969 when Strong's was taken over by Whitbread. The Bugle itself remains little changed externally apart from some modernisation to the signage. The shop to the left of the Bugle is now an Alldays convenience store and post office; the ironmongery has gone but the distinctive and attractive buildings are still recognisable. Also recognisable is what used to be Elcock's newsagent and tobacconist, although the premises are now Amanda's beauty salon. The increase in traffic along the A334 road means that a pelican crossing is now needed, but the provision of bench seats and heritage-style street lighting, together with a stricter definition of the car parking area, all helps to ensure that Botley retains a very pleasant ambience. *Classic Pictures/CH*

BISHOP'S WALTHAM STATION: The 3½-mile-long branch line from Botley to Bishop's Waltham was opened on 1 June 1863. It was originally intended that the line would continue to Droxford and Petersfield, but these plans did not come to fruition. When the line opened a temporary terminus was provided, but this was replaced in 1865 by the Italianate building seen in the 'past' photograph, which was built by the local Blanchard's Brickworks; notice the elaborate use of various types of bricks, which was clearly intended to display the Company's products. The 'past' photograph dates from around 1910 and is especially interesting in that it shows a single-carriage steam 'railmotor' of a type that provided the passenger service on the branch between 1905 and around 1915.

This short branch line was an early candidate for rationalisation, and passenger services were withdrawn in January 1933. Nonetheless freight traffic continued until April 1962, and apart from the loss of the canopy around 1960 the station remained largely intact until this final closure. The track was lifted and the buildings demolished in the mid-1960s, and a roundabout linking with a bypass road has been built on the site of the old station. Looking at the 'present' photograph, taken on Saturday 19 May 2001 from the same point as the 1910 view, it appears at first sight that no evidence remains that the railway once served Bishop's Waltham. However, turning the camera through 180 degrees and looking towards Botley along the former trackbed on the same date it can be seen that a pair of level crossing gates remain, while the story of the line is told on the information boards in the foreground. This part of the trackbed is now a public footpath, and provides a section of the Hampshire Millennium Pilgrims' Trail linking Portsmouth with Winchester. *Classic Pictures/CH(2)*

EAST MEON: The bus route from Southampton to Petersfield includes a delightful run through the scenic Meon Valley. Numbered Service 50 by Hants & Dorset, the route is now Solent Blue Line Service 52.

On 7 July 1970 Hants & Dorset fleet number 859 (UEL 733) stops to pick up a young lady passenger outside All Saints' Church, East Meon. This Bristol LS6G was originally delivered as a coach, but by 1970 was being used as a one-man-operated bus.

On the morning of Saturday 23 June 2001 the Solent Blue Line Service 52 journey at 08.55 from Southampton to Petersfield was operated by L510 EHD, a DAF with Ikarus bodywork legally owned by Marchwood Motorways, but operated under franchise to Solent Blue Line. On this occasion there were several passengers to pick up at East Meon Church, and the driver kindly waited while I took the photograph. It is pleasing to note that the churchyard looks much neater in 2001 than it did in 1970. The street lamp still supports a litter bin and would appear to be the same pole, but the lamp at the top has been replaced, by a replica of a more old-fashioned design! *M. J. Stephens (Peter Trevaskis collection)/CH*

PETERSFIELD SQUARE: For many years Hants & Dorset, Aldershot & District and Southdown buses all met at Petersfield. In the 'past' photograph we see Hants & Dorset fleet number 1483 (7683 LJ), a Bristol FL6G, about to leave Petersfield Square for Southampton on 30 March 1967. The 70-seat rear-entrance FL was the rarest of the Bristol F family, with only 45 being put in service nationwide out of a total production run of 2,275 Bristol F-series vehicles; Hants & Dorset had 12 of the 45, 7683 LJ being delivered new in 1962.

On Saturday 23 June 2001 a lively market was taking place in the Square, which on that warm summer morning was thronged with people. Trees have been planted, one of which conceals Cubitt & West's estate agency, which in fact looks very similar in 2001 to its appearance in 1967. On the left of the photograph it will be seen that the former Southdown Enquiry & Booking Office is now Saks hair and beauty salon, while Barclays Bank has been completely rebuilt in a modern style. In the background Boots can be seen occupying the same shop as in 1967. Note the youngsters with their mini-scooters in the 2001 view – the latest 'must have' craze, which I suspect will date the photograph quite accurately in years to come. *Aldershot & District Bus Interest Group/CH*

Lavant Street, Petersfield (showing Station)

LAVANT STREET, PETERSFIELD: In the 12th century the Lord of the Manor of Mapledurham planned a new town on part of his estate. A church was built, called St Peter's in the Field, and thus the town acquired its name. Over the centuries a thriving market town was built up in this attractive location near the Hampshire/Sussex border, with the wool and cloth trade having been especially important in days gone by. The railway came to Petersfield with the opening of the direct line from Waterloo to Portsmouth in January 1859. With the arrival of the railway, Lavant Street was laid out to provide a direct road link between the town centre and the station; the 'past' view, which dates from around 1910, is captioned 'Lavant Street (showing Station)'. The station can be seen in the background of both views, the 1859 buildings having survived virtually unchanged. When I took the 'present' photograph on Saturday 23 June 2001 the premises were very smartly turned out in South West Trains corporate identity.

The 1910 photograph has a genteel air about it. The shops on the left face some very middle class houses on the right-hand side of the road, complete with mature gardens that include some interesting topiary. Road users travel by foot or cycle – note the trade bicycle propped against the lamp-post in the left foreground.

Much has changed in 2001. Examination of the roofs and upper storeys of the buildings on the left proves that a number remain, although different retail trades are now carried on from the ground floors. The other side of the road has also been taken over for commercial use, with the consequent loss of the houses and gardens. Although a number of pedestrians can be seen on this lovely summer morning, the parked cars illustrate the revolution that has taken place in road transport over the years. *Classic Pictures/CH*

WICKHAM was the home of William of Wykeham, who founded Winchester College (hence old boys are known as Wykehamists) and New College, Oxford. It is likely that Wickham Square was laid out to accommodate the market, for which a charter was obtained in 1268. The Market no longer takes place, but the Square remains as one of the most attractive in Southern England. These photographs show the Square around 1905 and on 12 May 2001. As would be expected, the buildings at this historic location are easily recognisable, and most have changed very little. An exception is Commerce House, on the left of the 1905 view. This has been rebuilt as a taller structure, but is still a grocery and general stores, although now trading under the Co-op banner. It will also be noted that the four dormer windows have been removed from the roof of the King's Head Hotel. The trees are a welcome addition, and I suppose it is inevitable that the Square is nowadays used as a car park – which was well filled on the Saturday lunchtime when I took the 'present' photograph. Nonetheless this remains a delightful location, with a real sense of history remaining. *Classic Pictures/CH*

BRIDGE STREET, WICKHAM runs from the north end of the Square down to the A32 main road, and is seen here in the mid-1950s and on Saturday 12 May 2001. Again this is a very attractive location and there have been very few changes to the exteriors of the buildings. The parish church can be seen in the background of the 1950s view, which is in fact on the other side of the A32; note also the old-type 'Slow Major Road Ahead' sign.

The church is still there, but is now completely obscured by trees, which also conceal another significant feature. In front of the church it is possible in the 'past' photograph to discern the embankment of the Meon Valley railway line. This opened on 1 June 1903, and was designed to main-line standards, including spacious stations with capacity for ten-carriage trains. Provision was made for double track, although in the event only a single line was ever laid and the line was used almost exclusively by local trains. Closure to passengers came in 1955 after just over 50 years of use. However, the section between Wickham and Droxford was leased by a Mr Ashby for the purpose of evaluating a type of railcar that he hoped to develop. The rails here were lifted in the early 1970s and sections of the trackbed are now used as a footpath and cycleway. It will be noted that the school sign in the foreground has disappeared; Wickham CE Primary School has now been relocated, although the section of the A32 near the church is still known as School Road. *Classic Pictures/CH*

RAILWAY STATION AND TRAM TERMINUS, FAREHAM.

FAREHAM STATION opened with the line from Eastleigh to Gosport in November 1841 and the canopied building seen in the background of both of these photographs dates from that time. The line to Portsmouth opened in 1848, followed by that to Netley in 1889 and lastly to Alton via the Meon Valley in 1903. The line to Gosport was closed to passengers in 1953, as was the Meon Valley route in 1955, but the Southampton-Portsmouth and Eastleigh-Fareham lines were electrified in 1990.

Trams operated by Gosport & Fareham Tramways ran between Fareham Station and Gosport from 1905 until 1929. The 'past' photograph dates from around 1925, and one of the open-top cars that provided a 15-minute headway on the route can be seen on the extreme right of the picture. The Act of Parliament that allowed the abandonment of the tramway in 1929 also enabled the undertaking to become the Gosport & Fareham Omnibus Company, which continued as an independent bus operator in the area (trading as Provincial) until taken over by Hants & Dorset in 1970.

The Railway Hotel can be seen between the tram and the station in the 1925 photograph. This was demolished in the 1950s; the box-like replacement building has traded under several titles, but in 2001 is a public house called Prague Junction. The brick-arch railway bridge seen in the 'past' photograph was replaced in 1968 when the road was widened. A steady stream of traffic can be seen heading west towards Southampton in the early afternoon of Saturday 12 May 2001. *Classic Pictures/CH*

WEST STREET, FAREHAM.

WEST STREET, FAREHAM: When the 'past' photograph was taken in 1947 West Street was part of the main A27 road through Fareham. Prominent in the right foreground is the Savoy Cinema, built in 1933 and now replaced by the relocated branch of Woolworths. I wonder what a modern Health & Safety Officer would make of the girl standing on a chair adjusting the shop blind! Immediately beyond the Savoy Cinema the contemporary Savoy Parade survives in 2001. The large building behind this in the 'past' view is the Embassy Cinema, built in 1938 and demolished in 1983; in 2001 there is a McDonalds fast food restaurant on the site. Part of Fareham's Bus Station as originally built (see also pages 81 and 82) can be seen in the left foreground. In this view a Southdown double-deck bus is on Service 45 to Warsash and is thus parked by the departure stands normally used by Hants & Dorset. The bus station sign carries the pre-1948-style Hants & Dorset fleet name, and behind it the rather imposing Wesleyan Chapel was demolished in the early 1950s to allow the bus station to be extended – see opposite.

The relocation of the bus station and the demolition of Jeffreys furniture shop in 1993 has opened up the view of Westbury Manor in the 'present' photograph. Acquired by Fareham Council in 1932, the building is now used as a museum. The re-routing of the A27 along Western Way and Eastern Way in the late 1960s has enabled a section of West Street to be pedestrianised in recent years. The ornate street lamps in the 1947 view will be noted; the street lighting seen in the 2001 photograph is even more unusual and is accompanied by various items of modern art. When I took this photograph at lunchtime on Saturday 12 May 2001 a Leyland National bus, retired from PCV duties, was in use as a promotional vehicle for Fareham College and can be seen just behind the 'Dinky Donuts' stall. *Classic Pictures/CH*

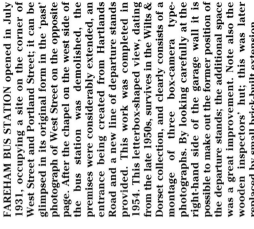

FAREHAM BUS STATION opened in July 1931, occupying a site on the corner of West Street and Portland Street; it can be glimpsed in its original form in the 'past' photograph of West Street on the opposite page. After the chapel on the west side of the bus station was demolished, the premises were considerably extended, an entrance being created from Hartlands Road and a new line of departure stands provided. This work was completed in 1954. This letterbox-shaped view, dating from the late 1950s, survives in the Wilts & Dorset collection, and clearly consists of a montage of three box-camera type-photographs. By looking carefully at the right-hand side of the garage wall it is possible to make out the former position of the departure stands; the additional space was a great improvement. Note also the wooden inspectors' hut; this was later replaced by small brick-built extension.

The scene looks very different in May 2001. A car park stands on the old bus station site, and a replacement bus station has been provided in Hartlands Road (see next page). The pedestrianisation of West Street can again be seen in the foreground, eliminating the need for the zebra crossing.
Wilts & Dorset collection/CH

FAREHAM BUS STATION: These two photographs, dating from 13 July 1956 and 12 May 2001 were taken from the same point; the location is fixed by the roof of the Church of the Sacred Heart, seen in the right background of both views.

In 1956 the area was part of the approach to the bus station from Hartlands Road, and two single-deckers are parked beside the garage wall. The front vehicle is of particular interest – fleet number 646 (GRU 855) was the first new coach received by Hants & Dorset after the Second World War, being the first of a batch of five delivered in July 1947. It is a Bristol L5G with Beadle bodywork and was delivered in the coach livery (see also page 91), but in October 1953 it was downgraded to dual-purpose status and is seen here in the green bus livery. Behind 646 is a standard Bristol single-deck bus with an Eastern Coach Works body also dating from the late 1940s.

Fareham's new bus station was officially opened on Monday 25 October 1993, and on the afternoon of Saturday 12 May 2001 Solent Blue Line Leyland Olympian No 729 (H729DDL) was the solitary double-deck bus among various single-deck types operated by First. *Aldershot & District Bus Interest Group/CH*

Transport of delight

LEYLAND TD3 DOUBLE-DECK BUSES: During its early years Hants & Dorset standardised on Leylands for its double-deck buses, purchasing more than 140 vehicles of this type before the final pre-war example was delivered in April 1937. These photographs show two Leyland TD3 buses that were both delivered new in April 1936.

BLJ 944 was photographed on Wednesday 12 August 1953, by which time its original Brush 53-seat lowbridge body had been overhauled by Eastern Coach Works in May 1942 and rebuilt by Portsmouth Aviation in August 1949. It was withdrawn from service in October 1954 and sold to a showman.

BLJ 955 had its original Leyland 7.6-litre petrol engine replaced by a Gardner 5LW diesel unit in March 1938, while the 53-seat Brush lowbridge body was extensively rebuilt in Hants & Dorset's own workshops during November 1947. This bus was withdrawn from service in September 1954 and also sold to a showman; it was observed still with a fair at Rotherhithe in February 1960. *Both Brian Jackson collection*

1949

BRISTOL K5G DOUBLE-DECK BUSES: As a Tilling company it was inevitable that Hants & Dorset's vehicle purchasing policy would be changed to favour Bristol rather than Leyland buses, and here we see two representatives of the Company's first batch of Bristol double-deck buses.

BTR 305 was received in May 1938, and was photographed towards the end of its life, parked out of service at Southampton on 26 June 1959. Its original high radiator has been replaced by the lower post-war type, while the lowbridge body was completely rebuilt in Hants & Dorset's own bodyshop in July 1947.

BTR 312 was delivered to Hants & Dorset in June 1938, and was given an entirely new Eastern Coach Works 55-seat lowbridge body in June 1949 together with the lower radiator; at a quick glance this bus therefore looks like a post-war vehicle. After withdrawal by Hants & Dorset, BTR 312 was purchased by Premier Travel of Cambridge, entering service with that operator in May 1960. It was photographed looking extremely smart wearing Premier Travel's blue livery at Drummer Street in Cambridge on 4 August 1961. This bus remained in service with Premier Travel until February 1965. *Both Aldershot & District Bus Interest Group*

A COUPLE OF GUYS: Although Southampton Corporation had an extensive fleet of Guy Arab buses (see also page 86), Hants & Dorset only operated nine vehicles of this type, all of which entered the fleet in 1942-3 as a wartime allocation by the Ministry of Transport. All were fitted with Gardner 5LW engines and spent most of their time with Hants & Dorset based at Eastleigh Depot.

The first Guy to arrive was FRU 7, delivered in September 1942 with a Strachen 55-seat lowbridge body. The body was rebuilt by Reading of Portsmouth in November 1948, and the bus is seen here in the early 1950s in rebuilt condition. Withdrawn in September 1953, FRU 7 was sold to a showman in eastern England and was still travelling with the fair ten years later.

The penultimate vehicle of the batch, DCR 868, carried a 55-seat lowbridge body by Roe when new in April 1943. This was rebuilt by Portsmouth Aviation in September 1949, and the bus is seen in Eastleigh on 12 August 1953 operating a Service 115 journey to Romsey. Withdrawn by Hants & Dorset in September 1955, DCR 868 saw further service with the fleet of T. D. Alexander of Sheffield. *Both Brian Jackson collection*

1944

THE CAVE BROWNE CAVE SYSTEM: In the late 1940s an experimental heating and ventilation system for buses was developed at Southampton University by Wing Commander T. R. Cave Browne Cave. This used piped heat from the engine to warm up air admitted through radiators at destination screen level. Depending on weather conditions, the warm air could be delivered to the saloons or discharged through side vents as appropriate.

The maroon and cream Guy Arab buses operated by Southampton Corporation were a familiar sight in that city for more than 20 years. Fleet number 162 (FTR 509), delivered new in 1949 with a Park Royal 60-seat highbridge body, became in 1951 the first bus in the country to be fitted with the Cave Browne Cave system. A member of staff is seen looking at the converted bus with what may be best described as wary curiosity! The Cave Browne Cave equipment was removed from FTR 509 in December 1963, but the bus remained in service until April 1967, when it was disposed of for scrap.

The first Hants & Dorset bus to be fitted with Cave Browne Cave equipment was fleet number 1068 (APR 423), a Bristol K5G dating from 1940 and fitted with an Eastern Coach Works 55-seat lowbridge body. The system was fitted in 1953, and the photograph shows the vehicle at Southampton in September of that year. As well as the unusual frontal appearance, the style of the 1940 bodywork can be contrasted with GLJ 970 on the left, a K5G dating from November 1947, and KEL 703 (right), a K6B new in July 1950.

The experiments with the Cave Browne Cave equipment were successful; after further trials on some Bristol LD vehicles in 1956, the system was offered by Bristol/ECW as an option for the Lodekka family from the late 1950s onwards, and buses with the Cave Browne Cave system became a familiar sight in many areas of Britain. *Both Brian Jackson Collection*

POST-WAR LOWBRIDGE DOUBLE-DECK BUSES: Unsurprisingly for a Tilling company, Hants & Dorset took delivery of a large number of double-deck buses from the Bristol K family with 55-seat lowbridge bodywork by Eastern Coach Works in the years after the Second World War. However, the unique circumstances of the late 1940s resulted in some non-standard vehicles also coming into the fleet. In January 1948 the Company took delivery of seven Leyland PD1A buses with 55-seat Eastern Coach Works lowbridge bodies. These vehicles were to become particularly associated with the routes between Winchester and Southampton, and fleet number 1149 (GLJ 961) is seen at Winchester Bus Station on 30 December 1955 ready to operate to Southampton on Service 47. Being non-standard, this batch of vehicles had a relatively short life with Hants & Dorset; GLJ 961 was taken out of service in August 1963.

In contrast, the second photograph epitomises the standard Tilling group purchase of that era. Fleet number 1290 (KRU 956) is a Bristol KSW6B delivered in September 1951 with the usual 55-seat lowbridge body by Eastern Coach Works. On 4 May 1956 this bus was at Southampton Bus Station on Service 60 to Romsey. Buses of this type continued in service with Hants & Dorset until well into the 1970s; KRU 956 was withdrawn in November 1972.
Aldershot & District Bus Interest Group (2)

HIGHBRIDGE INTERLUDE: Because of low railway bridges on many of its routes, most double-deck buses purchased by Hants & Dorset prior to the early 1950s were of the lowbridge type with a sunken side gangway on the upper deck. However, a general shortage of buses in the late 1940s, exacerbated in Hants & Dorset's case by the temporary diversion of 39 of its new Bristol K6As to London Transport for a year, caused the Company to take delivery of more non-standard buses during 1949. Among them were six Leyland Titan PD2/1 buses with Leyland 56-seat highbridge bodywork, which were originally intended for export to South Africa. They spent their time with Hants & Dorset allocated to Southampton depot, where they were normally employed on the routes to the Waterside area, as exemplified by this photograph of fleet number 1222 (JEL 499) at Southampton Bus Station in September 1953. All six of these buses were withdrawn in 1962 and disposed of for scrap.

During 1951 Hants & Dorset switched to highbridge bodies for its ongoing delivery of Bristol KSW/Eastern Coach Works double-deck buses. Most of the 1951 intake went to the Company's Western Area, where they were

associated with the Poole town network of routes for well over 20 years, but a number of the final KSWs delivered in 1952 worked in Hants & Dorset's Eastern Area. One such was fleet number 1323 (LRU 52), seen in the background at Southampton operating a Service 36 journey to Hammonds Green on 13 August 1961. Highbridge Bristol KSWs continued in service with Hants & Dorset until November 1974.

In front of LRU 52, Bristol FS6G No 1453 (5680 EL) on Service 37 to Salisbury was almost new when the photograph was taken, having been delivered in June 1961. This was one of the first Hants & Dorset buses to have fluorescent interior lighting, and also displays a short-lived feature of 1960s buses – the illuminated exterior advertisement panel. 5680 EL was withdrawn in December 1976. *Brian Jackson collection/Aldershot & District Bus Interest Group*

LODEKKA DEVELOPMENTS: Although I liked lowbridge buses with their four-across upstairs seating (and yes, I did work on them as a conductor at Poole), most people found the layout awkward, and when the Bristol Lodekka was developed, offering a low-height bus with a centre gangway on both decks, it was immediately adopted as a standard by most of the Tilling group. Hants & Dorset was no exception, with all new double-deckers purchased between 1953 and 1968 being from the Bristol Lodekka family and carrying (of course) Eastern Coach Works bodies. A typical example is fleet number 1405 (UEL 726), one of the 1957 intake, which is seen outside Southampton Bus Station on 8 April 1962 while operating on Service 88 between Tatwin Crescent and Southampton Central Station.

The Lodekka was originally designed as a 27-feet-long vehicle, but from July 1956 the maximum length for double-deck buses was increased to 30 feet. The first six Lodekkas of this length were built in 1957; one was allocated to Hants & Dorset as fleet number 1406 (UEL 727) and delivered in October of that year. Photographed departing from Southampton Bus Station for Lepe Beach on 20 July 1967, this rare vehicle can be compared with UEL 726 in the view above. The extra length allowed the seating capacity to be increased by ten to 70. In 1959 the first F-series Bristol Lodekkas began to appear, and a 70-seat rear-entrance version was available (see page 75), but most operators who required a 70-seat vehicle opted for the forward-entrance FLF. *Both Aldershot & District Bus Interest Group*

SINGLE-DECK MISCELLANY: For many years Hants & Dorset provided a bus service between Southampton Central Station and the Royal Pier, timed to provide connections between the London trains and the ferries to and from the Isle of Wight. The vehicle seen operating this service on a September evening in 1953 is interesting. Fleet number 644 (CCR 856) was taken into service in February 1939 as a coach. In August 1950 it was rebuilt as a 20-seat service bus and painted in the green bus livery. It was certainly carrying a full load on this occasion – no doubt the passengers were grateful for the fresh air from the half-drop windows! Withdrawn by Hants & Dorset in November 1956, CCR 856 became a mobile shop in Bradford and subsequently a café at Ilkley. This experimental conversion of a coach to a service bus proved very successful, and during the 1950s and 1960s many coaches that were no longer in their first flush of youth were converted into buses to extend their working lives – see also pages 74 and 82.

The maximum length for a single-deck bus was increased to 30 feet from 1 June 1950, and the first Hants & Dorset buses to take advantage of the new length were three Bristol saloons with 36-seat rear-entrance dual-purpose bodywork by Portsmouth Aviation. This trio remained as crew-operated buses throughout their service with the Company. Fleet number 780 (KLJ 750) is seen at Southampton Bus Station on 4 June 1961, together with fleet number 792 (LRU 66), an underfloor-engined Bristol LS5G new in November 1953 that had been converted for one-man operation in September 1958. KLJ 750 was withdrawn in November 1965, while LRU 66 remained in service until March 1970. *Brian Jackson collection/Aldershot & District Bus Interest Group*

THE POST-WAR COACHING SCENE: With a public eager to resume peacetime travelling habits, but with new motor cars very difficult to obtain and petrol still rationed, Hants & Dorset had an urgent need for new coaches in the late 1940s. Between July 1947 and August 1950 the Company brought into service 39 Bristol L coaches with bodywork variously by Beadle, Dutfield and Portsmouth Aviation. Forming the backbone of the coaching fleet during this extremely busy period, this intake of vehicles is exemplified by fleet number 658 (JEL 98), a Beadle-bodied L6B dating from March 1949, which is seen laying over at Southsea while operating an afternoon tour on 9 August 1956. JEL 98 was subsequently rebuilt as a full-fronted bus in December 1957 and withdrawn in November 1961.

Fleet number 728 (ARU 183) was, as implied by its registration, a rather older vehicle. It was the last of a batch of 14 Leyland TS7 coaches purchased by Hants & Dorset in 1935, and when new carried a 32-seat Beadle coach body. The entire batch of 14 was requisitioned by the War Department in 1940, and ARU 183 was one of three repurchased by Hants & Dorset in late 1948. Having seen war service the Beadle coach bodies were in a very indifferent state and were replaced in September 1949 by Portsmouth Aviation 32-seat rear-entrance dual-

purpose bodies. Painted in bus livery when first rebodied, 728 was repainted in the cream coach livery seen here in May 1952, subsequently reverting to bus livery in November 1953. Despite being to all intents and purposes a coach, it would appear to have recently arrived from Romsey on Service 63 when this photograph was taken in Southampton during September 1953. The unusual brackets fixed to the roof will be noted; this vehicle was sometimes used on private hire duties for a rowing club and special racks were fitted to these brackets to enable their boats to be carried. This interesting vehicle was withdrawn in September 1956 and subsequently worked for a contractor until its demise in a Tees-side scrapyard. *Aldershot & District Bus Interest Group/Brian Jackson collection*

A TOUCH OF THE BLUES: Royal Blue Coaches were a familiar sight in the West Country until their routes were subsumed into the National Express network in the 1970s. In their day a very popular means of travel, Royal Blue coaches were also very much part of the Southampton scene, with coaches on the busy Bournemouth-London and Bournemouth-Portsmouth routes passing through the city. These two photographs, showing coaches outside the Hants & Dorset bus garage in Grosvenor Square (see also page 10), were both taken on Monday 7 September 1953.

Fleet number 1201 (JUO 933) is a Bristol L6B dating from 1948 with a 31-seat coach body by Beadle to the traditional half-cab design. In 1958 this body was removed and the chassis lengthened to 30 feet. A new Eastern Coach Works full fronted bus body was then fitted, and in this guise the vehicle gave a further 11 years' service to Southern National.

Fleet number 1284 (LTA 872) was photographed at 6pm while operating the 2.15pm journey from London to

Bournemouth, where it was due to arrive at 7.21pm. This coach was new in 1952 and was one of Royal Blue's first batch of underfloor-engined Bristol LS6G vehicles. The Eastern Coach Works body seated 41 passengers. Later coaches of this type had a revised windscreen arrangement that eliminated the curved corner windows, which were a source of distracting reflections for drivers at night. Notice also the luggage rack on the roof, a distinctive feature of Royal Blue coaches delivered up to 1953, but omitted from vehicles introduced thereafter. LTA 872 was withdrawn from Royal Blue service in 1968 and passed through a dealer to Shepardson of Barton on Humber, then to Allenways of Birmingham before being scrapped in 1971. *Both Brian Jackson Collection*

WHEN KING ALFRED REIGNED:
The bus services operated by the King Alfred fleet have already been mentioned elsewhere in the book, and no chapter looking at transport in the area would be complete without reference to this once renowned company. Winchester businessman Robert Chisnell had started a taxi service during the First World War, and by 1920 was also running charabanc excursions. Stage carriage bus operations started on 9 October 1922 with routes from Winchester Broadway to Stanmore, Shawford and Twyford, Battery Hill Corner and Flowerdown. Expansion and consolidation through the 1920s and 1930s saw King Alfred buses running to Sparsholt, Stockbridge, Broughton, Hookpit, Sutton Scotney and Basingstoke by the outbreak of the Second World War. By this time Mr Chisnell's sons Fred and Bob were largely responsible for running the business, and Mr Chisnell senior died, in his mid-70s, on 5 June 1945.

Prior to the Second World War King Alfred had operated a single-deck fleet, its first double-deck bus being a Leyland Titan TD7, delivered in March 1942 with 55-seat lowbridge utility bodywork by Brush. Four lowbridge-bodied Guy Arabs followed between November 1942 and November 1944, but after the war the Leyland Titan became the standard choice for new King Alfred double-deck buses for the next ten years. Four Leyland-bodied 53-seat lowbridge PD1As were received during 1947, followed by five 56-seat highbridge PD2/1s, also with Leyland bodies, between May 1949 and September 1951. A further five PD2s with Leyland lowbridge bodywork had entered service by July 1953. The last two Leyland Titans were taken into stock in October 1956; these were PD2/24s with 55-seat lowbridge bodies by East Lancs, which incorporated the concealed-radiator 'tin front' look then fashionable. The first of the pair was POU 494, which was in

service with King Alfred until October 1972. This bus was preserved after withdrawal and these photographs were taken on Sunday 16 April 2000 at a Wessex Transport Society Running Day – I travelled on it from Bournemouth to Poole and was reminded of journeys on King Alfred buses as a teenager in the 1960s.

The early post-war years had perhaps marked the zenith of the King Alfred operation. By the 1960s staff shortages and traffic congestion caused increasing problems, which intensified in the early 1970s, by which time the Chisnell brothers wished to retire. The last day of service for King Alfred buses was Saturday 28 April 1973, the routes thereafter being operated by Hants & Dorset. *All CH*

SOUTHAMPTON'S TRAMS: The first tram route in Southampton opened on 5 May 1879. It was operated by the Southampton Tramways Company and ran between the Floating Bridge (see page 60) and Portswood. A route to Shirley was added from 9 June 1879. These trams were all horse-drawn, but in 1898 the tramways were taken over by Southampton Corporation, which proceeded to electrify the network. The first route to be thus modernised was that to Shirley, which was electrified from January 1900. The tram system was subsequently extended, reaching Northam in 1910, Bassett in 1921, Swaythling in 1922 and Bitterne via Cobden Bridge in 1923, with the final link along Burgess Road between Bassett and Swaythling being opened in 1930.

The need for trams to pass through the Bargate (not avoided until much later – see page 14) restricted both the height and the width of the vehicles. All of the initial electric tram cars were open-topped. The lower deck had longitudinal seating along its sides as then normal in trams, while the upper deck had a 'knifeboard' back-to-back bench seat along the centre. Car 39, one of a batch built by Hurst, Nelson & Co in 1903-4, is seen on the Shirley route in its original condition. Cars delivered from 1909 onwards had their upper decks extended as canopies to the car ends, and many of the earlier cars were subsequently modified to match.

Later Southampton Corporation built its own tram cars at its Portswood works, and between 1923 and 1932 a number of specially designed and fully enclosed domed-roofed trams, which could run through the Bargate, were produced. These incorporated standard reversible two-by-two seating on the top deck.

Although these modern enclosed trams replaced most of the earlier stock, a number of the open-top 'knifeboard' trams did remain in service. One such was car 45, another of the Hurst, Nelson & Co batch and identical to car 39 when first delivered but later rebuilt with longer canopies as described above. Withdrawn in 1948, this tram was sold to the Light Railway Transport League for £10. After nine years in store at Blackpool, car

45 was then exhibited for a while at the Montagu Motor Museum, Beaulieu. In October 1960 it was moved to Crich in Derbyshire, where over the years it has received loving care and attention in the workshops of the National Tramway Museum, and on occasions it is still possible to take a ride on car 45 along the demonstration track. This photograph, taken during a visit on Wednesday 2 August 2000, shows car 45 at work. Tramway operation in Southampton ended on 31 December 1949. *David Harvey collection/CH*

GATEWAY TO THE WORLD: Already a significant port in medieval times, Southampton's extensive docks were developed from the 19th century onwards, taking advantage of the area's double tides. In the days of the great international liners Southampton was known as 'The Gateway to the World'. One of the most remarkable structures during this period was a massive floating dry dock, brought into use in 1924. The opening of the King George V Graving Dock in the mid-1930s reduced the need for the floating dry dock, and it was removed in 1940.

These photographs show two famous liners in the floating dock. In the first view we see RMS *Aquitania*, which was launched from the Clydebank shipyard of John Brown in April 1913. When built she was the largest vessel in the Cunard fleet, and operated with *Mauretania* and *Lusitania* on the North Atlantic service. During the First World War she was used as an armed merchant cruiser and a hospital ship as well as for troop transport. Converted to burn oil following war service, she continued her North Atlantic duties, and from 1936 onwards her partner was *Queen Mary*. *Aquitania* was due to be retired with the introduction of *Queen Elizabeth* in 1940, but the Second World War gave her an extra lease of life as a troop-ship. The severe shortage of shipping in the immediate post-war period saw her return to the North Atlantic run, eventually sailing to the breakers in 1949. In her 36-year career *Aquitania* sailed more than 3 million miles and her passing marked the end of the great four-funnel liners that had once been so much part of the Southampton scene.

The second view shows RMS *Berengaria*. This ship was launched in May 1912 from the Hamburg shipyard Vaalkan Werke as the *Imperator* for the German Hamburg-Amerika Line. Handed over to the Allies in 1919 under the reparations agreement, she was placed with Cunard and renamed *Berengaria* after the wife of King Richard the Lionheart. She also served on the Atlantic run until the introduction of *Queen Mary* in 1936, when she was taken to Barrow and broken up. *Both F. G. O. Stuart (Brian Jackson collection)*

Index of locations